WALLY'S STORIES

WALLY'S STORIES

Vivian Gussin Paley

Harvard University Press
Cambridge, Massachusetts
and London, England
1981

Library of Congress Cataloging in Publication Data

Paley, Vivian Gussin, 1929-
  Wally's stories.

  1. Kindergarten—Methods and manuals.
2. Creative thinking   (Education) I. Title.
LB1169.P24   372.13′078   80-21882
ISBN 0-674-94592-1

For Irving, David, Bobby
and my mother
Yetta Meisel Gussin

Foreword

Courtney B. Cazden

This book doesn't need a long foreword. Vivian Paley is such a sensitive observer and writer that her kindergarten children speak delightfully and wisely for themselves. But hers is an unusual classroom, and *Wally's Stories* is about only one part of its life.

The "stories" are of several kinds. Some are made up by Wally and his classmates, some are picture books and fairy tales. All are read, reread, and acted out again and again. Others are five-year-old discussions of very serious topics— like whether stones melt when they are boiled. When you are five, there is much in the world that needs to be accounted for, and these accounts are "stories" to us adults when children prefer their magical explanations to those we call "true."

Teachers are usually counseled to respond to such stories with some version of what might be called "confrontation pedagogy": rub the children's minds in the errors of their thoughts by providing arguments against their inconsistencies and evidence that magic doesn't work. Although that advice seems plausible, there is reason to believe that this approach is more comforting to the adult than helpful to the child.

Language—the aspect of child development I know best— is a case in point. There are times during all children's preschool years when their advancing knowledge of language as a rule-governed system produces words like *goed* and *holded*, and (in answer to the question, "What are you doing?") utterances like "I doing dancing." At those moments, the child seems impervious to contradiction, and no amount of adult correction has any obvious effect.

As with language, so too in the classroom. Instead of confrontation, it may be more useful for teachers to go beyond their own adult egocentricity and explore the ideas that flow from the children's own premises. That is what Paley has done, with rich gains in language and behavior in this five-year-old community. And that is the part of its life that *Wally's Stories* is about. Between the lines of the revealing, sometimes poignant episodes, one catches glimpses of the teacher's complex role—supporting the children in their imagined worlds and providing firm anchor points to a more stable "reality" as well.

Prologue

Imagine an enormous turnip in a row of ordinary turnips. Grandfather tries but fails to pull it up. Grandmother comes to help, but together they cannot do it. First a grandchild and then a black cat join the others, but the turnip stays firm. Only when a brown mouse adds his effort does it come up.

How can a tiny mouse make such a difference? Common sense insists that the turnip is ready to come up, and the mouse only appears to make the big difference. But in a kindergarten classroom the appearance is as good as the deed.

No—better than the deed. When a magical idea is presented, the common-sense approach is looked at but then discarded. Hear five-year-olds who have just entered kindergarten as they discuss *The Tale of the Turnip*.

Teacher:	Why did the turnip come up when the little brown mouse pulled?
Warren:	Because the grandfather and grandmother couldn't pull it up.
Teacher:	They couldn't. You're right. Then the mouse helped and it came up. Why?
Warren:	He was stronger.
Deana:	If all of them pulled, the enormous turnip *would* come up.

Wally:	That was only the strength they needed.
Eddie:	If just some pulled it wouldn't. But they needed all to pull.
Wally:	Maybe the mouse lived down there.
Jill:	Under the turnip? Is that where he lives at night?
Wally:	Maybe he pushed it up when it was coming out.
Jill:	Maybe he was stronger than they were.
Eddie:	Animals could be stronger than people.
Deana:	Maybe the roots got stuck to the bottom of the ground and when the mouse came he could pull the roots up.
Fred:	If the cat and mouse pulled theirselves it comes up.
Teacher:	Why?
Fred:	They're stronger. But if the roots stuck they might need help.
Wally:	Maybe someone was inside the dirt and he saw the roots and he pulled it so they couldn't pull the turnip.
Tanya:	If the mouse pulled it up by himself it would work.
Wally:	What if two people were underneath pulling?
Teacher:	How would they happen to be under the ground?
Eddie:	They dug a hole.
Tanya:	But the mouse has the most power. Right? (*Everyone agrees.*)

The mouse's size is not important. A mouse can push up a huge turnip because the child can see him do it in his mind. The child can also see the other story characters pulling on

the turnip, but he would rather think about the mouse. Fine.
Unless you are a teacher determined to teach the concepts
that are in *your* mind. How does one approach a lesson on
the wheel, for example, when children prefer to believe that it
is easier to move an entire basket of wood than to move a
small piece?

Teacher:	Watch me try to move this heavy basket. Uh . . . this is really heavy. I'm getting out of breath.
Eddie:	I can do it easy. (*Straining and tugging, he moves it an inch.*) I can do it easy.
Teacher:	You did get red in the face. Does anyone think that looked so easy?
Everyone:	Yes.
Teacher:	Okay. Look, here's the problem. Can anyone figure out an easy way to move the basket over to the woodbench?
Deana:	With my feet. (*She pushes her feet against the basket but it does not move.*) These are the wrong shoes. I can do it easy with my other shoes.
Wally:	I can pick it up. (*He winces as he scrapes his nails on the rough wood but lifts part of the basket perhaps half an inch.*) There! That was easy.
Teacher:	Wally, could you bring me a piece of wood from the woodbox? (*He runs over and returns with a small piece.*) Was that easy or hard?
Wally:	Easy.
Teacher:	If *that* was easy, would you say moving the basket is easy or hard?
Wally:	Easy. Real easy. I could do it with my head too. You want to see?

Months will pass before we "invent" the wheel. Meanwhile there are other questions: Can Wally become a mother lion? Who stole the lima beans that did not come up? Can a witch be invisible? Is there a black Santa? Does Tanya have the right to disturb the Ella Jenkins record? This is high drama in the kindergarten. The children care enough about these subjects to tell us what they really think. My purpose is to uncover and describe this remarkable point of view.

Wally:	People don't feel the same as grown-ups.
Teacher:	Do you mean "Children don't"?
Wally:	Because grown-ups don't remember when they were little. They're already an old person. Only if you have a picture of you doing that. Then you could remember.
Eddie:	But not thinking.
Wally:	You never can take a picture of thinking. Of course not.

You can, however, write a book about thinking—by recording the conversations, stories, and playacting that take place as events and problems are encountered. A wide variety of thinking emerges, as morality, science, and society share the stage with fantasy. If magical thinking seems most conspicuous, it is because it is the common footpath from which new trails are explored. I have learned not to resist this magic but to seek it out as a legitimate part of "real" school.

Wally's Stories follows a group of five-year-olds through their kindergarten year. The scene is the classroom, and the teacher is the stage manager (additional stage directions are in the appendix). The children are scriptwriters and actors who know what kindergartners want to say.

Wally

"He did that on purpose! You knocked my tower down on purpose!" Fred grabs Wally's leg and begins to cry.

Wally pushes Fred away. "I'm a dinosaur. I'm smashing the city."

"You didn't ask me. You have to ask." The tears have stopped.

"Dinosaurs don't ask."

I swoop down, dinosaurlike, and order Wally to the time-out chair. This will give me a ten-minute respite from his fantasies. His quick smile that is a silent laugh and his laugh that is a lion's roar are gone. He stares past me at the window, hunched over on the chair. Wally has come to our school after two and a half years in a day-care center. Nothing in the school report suggests the scope of his imagination. It is a customary "bad boy" report: restless, hyperative, noisy, uncooperative. Tonight the children will give their mothers a similar description: there's a boy Wally who growls like a lion; the teacher yells at him but not at me.

"Are you being bad, Wally?" asks Rose. Rose is from the same day-care center as Wally, and she once told me that he got spanked there every day.

"Were you bad, Wally?" she asks again.

"I was a dinosaur."

"Oh."

Wally cannot understand why I don't admire him when he is a dinosaur. Before he goes home he'll ask me if he was good. He has to tell his mother, and he is never sure. The time-out chair is not connected to his perception of events.

"Was I good today?" he asks. I am tying his shoes at the top of the outside steps.

"You were okay except for the playground."

"What did I do?"

"You knocked down that first-grade boy."

"The black boy? Jason? We were superheroes."

"You were too rough."

"He's still my friend."

Fred is still his friend, too. As Wally changes from dinosaur to superhero to lion, Fred keeps an eye on him. He examines Wally's behavior and then watches my reaction. Wally, however, never watches me. He seldom takes his cues from adults, bringing forth his own script for being a five-year-old. He is never bored, except when he's on the time-out chair, and even then his head dances with images and stories.

"Whoever sits in the time-out chair will die for six years until the magic spell is broken," he says one day after a session on the chair.

"They turn into a chair," Eddie decides, "and then God breaks the spell."

"Not God," corrects Wally. "God is for harder things."

"Fairies could do it," says Lisa. "Not the tooth kind."

"It *is* a fairy," Wally agrees. "The one for magic spells."

The children like Wally's explanations for events better than mine, so I give fewer and fewer interpretations each day and instead listen to Wally's. The familiar chord he strikes stimulates others to speak with candor, and I am the beneficiary. However, Wally does not always teach me what I want to learn. He is a lightning rod, attracting the teacher's negative sparks, keeping them from landing on others. It is a role that receives little credit.

"You're riding too fast, Wally," I caution.

"Okay."

"Don't crash into the wall."

"Okay."

"Do *not* slam into things, Wally!"

"I didn't see it."

When I begin to play the piano, he leaps over Lisa and Rose to get to the piano first, but before the song is finished he is on the outer edge of the rug, growling.

"Don't make that noise, Wally," I say.

"It's a warning growl."

"Not at piano time."

"I'm guarding the lions," he whispers. "The growl means I hear a suspicious noise." The children stop squirming and watch Wally as he crouches in concentration. Several boys copy his pose and give low growls.

One day at lunch Wally says, "I'm going to be a mother lion when I grow up."

"A mother lion?" I ask. "Can you become a mother lion?"

"Sure. The library has everything. Even magic. When I'm eight I can learn magic. That's how."

"Why a mother lion?"

"Because I would have babies and do the mommy work. They stay home and take care of babies. Daddy lions go to work and have to walk fast."

Deana has been listening. "People can't turn into animals."

"That's true," Wally says.

"You changed your mind, Wally?" I ask.

"It *is* true, what she said. But I'm going to use magic."

"Oh, I didn't hear him say that." Deana leans forward. "If he uses magic he might. Maybe. It's very hard to do."

Fred joins in. "I might become a daddy crocodile. Every time a person tries to kill them they can swat at their guns."

"Fred," I ask, "do you believe Wally can become a mother lion?"

"No. Only if he practices very hard."

Eddie and Lisa are in the doll corner when I bring up the subject. "Wally has decided to become a lion when he grows up." They look up and laugh hesitantly. "He intends to learn magic," I add.

"Oh, that way," says Eddie. "It depends how hard he studies. That's the hardest thing to do."

"It's impossible," Lisa argues. "You can't turn into a lion. That's too big. Maybe a mouse or a cat." She pauses. "But he can dress up to look like a lion."

I turn to Earl. "Do you suppose a boy could become a mother?"

"He can put on a dress and a wig," Earl answers.

"And a mask," says Lisa.

"How about a lion? Can Wally become a lion?"

"No," answers Earl. "He has to be a huge man with sideburns."

"What if he uses magic?"

"Oh, I thought you meant ordinary. He could do it with magic," says Earl.

"But it *would* be very hard," says Lisa.

The next day I ask Andy, "Do you think it's interesting to be a father?"

"Sure. If a robber comes, the father punches him in the nose."

"Wally wants to become a lion, Andy. What do you think?"

Andy is quiet for a moment. "He can't. Unless he becomes an actress. Or he can wish for it, and if God wants you to become that then you can do it. Wait. I'm not too sure about lions. I know he could become a smaller thing. But he could dress up like a lion."

"Would he *be* a lion if he dressed up like a lion?"

"I mean just until he learns to do that trick."

Wally frowns and squirms beside me on the playground bench. A hot flush gives his brown skin a reddish tone. His black curly hair is coated with sand, sweat, and dirt.

"You get into fights out here every day," I say. "You keep making me punish you."

"I don't care," he shrugs.

"I know you care. You'd rather be running around."

"I don't care."

Later he dictates a story.

> Once upon a time there was a little lion and he lived alone because his mother and father was dead and one day he went hunting and he saw two lions and they were his mother and father so he took his blanket to their den because it was bigger.

"But weren't the mother and father dead?" I ask. He has a quick answer. "They came alive again because he only thought they were dead. They really went out shopping and he didn't recognize them because they were wearing different clothes."

"Can I be the father in your story?" Fred asks. We usually acted out stories as soon as they were written and books as soon as they were read.

"Okay," says Wally. "Fred will be the father, Rose is the mother, I'm the little brother, and Eddie is the magician."

"There's no magician in your story," I remind Wally, who doesn't read yet.

"Yes, there is. I just didn't tell you about him."

A few days later a first-grade teacher complains about Wally.

"This is embarrassing," I tell Wally and the whole class. "I don't know what else to do about you, Wally."

"Just keep reminding him," says Lisa.

"But I continually warn him," I tell her.

"Remind him nicely."

"Lisa, he made you cry today."

"Keep telling Wally not to be rough," she says.

Eddie agrees. "Say to him, 'Be good, Wally, will you?' "

I turn to Wally. "Your classmates don't want you to be punished."

He smiles shyly. "That's because we're friends."

Stories

"Once there was a man and a mother and two sisters and a brother."

We are acting out Wally's newest story. He dictates three or four a week, never repeating a plot.

Story dictation had been a minor activity in my previous

kindergartens, even though books and dramatics had been high-priority activities. Few children chose to tell a story if they could do something else instead. For years I accepted the "fact" that no more than four or five children out of twenty-five enjoyed dictating stories, and most often they were girls.

I had asked last year's class about this.

Teacher:	Why do girls choose story dictating more than boys?
Sam:	Boys like to do Star Wars things—stuff like that. Girls like writing and listening to the teacher.
Robbie:	Boys like blocks and woodwork and superheroes.
Tom:	And guns and cars and tough things.
Sandy:	I was making a motorcycle. That's why I didn't come.
Della:	They think it's dull, sitting and coloring and telling things. Boys are rougher.
Teacher:	But boys like to listen to stories and act them out. Then why not dictate stories?
Robbie:	It's very hard to explain. I'm storing up energy because I have a cold. So I don't want to use up my energy writing stories.

The first time I asked Wally if he wanted to write a story he looked suprised. "You didn't teach me how to write yet," he said.

"You just tell *me* the story, Wally. I'll write the words."

"What should I tell about?"

"You like dinosaurs. You could tell about dinosaurs."

He dictated this story.

> The dinosaur smashed down the city and the people got mad and put him in jail.

"Is that the end?" I asked. "Did he get out?"

> He promised he would be good so they let him go home and his mother was waiting.

We acted out the story immediately for one reason—I felt sorry for Wally. He had been on the time-out chair twice that day, and his sadness stayed with me. I wanted to do something nice for him, and I was sure it would please him if we acted out his story.

It made Wally very happy, and a flurry of story writing began that continued and grew all year. The boys dictated as many stories as the girls, and we acted out each story the day it was written if we could.

Before, we had never acted out these stories. We had dramatized every other kind of printed word—fairy tales, story books, poems, songs—but it had always seemed enough just to write the children's words. Obviously it was not; the words did not sufficiently represent the action, which needed to be shared. For this alone, the children would give up play time, as it was a true extension of play.

To return to Wally's latest story.

> Once there was a man and a mother and two sisters and a brother. First the oldest sister ran away. Then the second sister decided to stay home with the father but he ran away too. So the little brother and the sister were left and she learned how to

cook. One day a lion came because she wished for a lion and also they lived in the jungle. He said, "Can I be your pet?" She said, "I was just wishing for a lion pet. You can carry us wherever you want." So they lived happily ever after.

Rulers

Rulers were another example of the wide gulf separating my beliefs from those the children demonstrated whenever they were allowed to follow their ideas to logical conclusions. I had not realized that "rulers are not really real." We were about to act out "Jack and the Beanstalk" when Wally and Eddie disagreed about the relative size of our two rugs.

Wally: The big rug is the giant's castle. The small one is Jack's house.

Eddie: Both rugs are the same.

Wally: They can't be the same. Watch me. I'll walk around the rug. Now watch— walk, walk, walk, walk, walk, walk, walk, walk, walk—count all these walks. Okay. Now count the other rug. Walk, walk, walk, walk, walk. See? That one has more walks.

Eddie: No fair. You cheated. You walked faster.

Wally: I don't have to walk. I can just look.

Eddie: I can look too. But you have to mea-
           sure it. You need a ruler. About six
           hundred inches or feet.
Wally: We have a ruler.
Eddie: Not that one. Not the short kind. You
           have to use the long kind that gets
           curled up in a box.
Wally: Use people. People's bodies. Lying
           down in a row.
Eddie: That's a great idea. I never even
           thought of that.

Wally announces a try-out for "rug measurers." He adds
one child at a time until both rugs are covered—four children
end to end on one rug and three on the other. Everyone is
satisfied, and the play continues with Wally as the giant on
the rug henceforth known as the four-person rug. The next
day Eddie measures the rugs again. He uses himself,Wally,
and two other childen. But this time they do not cover the
rug.

Wally: You're too short. I mean someone is
            too short. We need Warren. Where's
            Warren?
Teacher: He's not here today.
Eddie: Then we can't measure the rug.
Teacher: You can only measure the rug when
            Warren is here?
Jill: Because he's longer.
Deana: Turn everyone around. Then it will fit.
            *(Eddie rearranges the measurers so that each is now
            in a different position. Their total length is the
            same.)*
Eddie: No, it won't work. We have to wait for
            Warren.

Deana:	Let me have a turn. I can do it.
Jill:	You're too big, Deana. Look at your feet sticking out. Here's a rule. Nobody bigger than Warren can measure the rug.
Fred:	Wait. Just change Ellen and Deana because Ellen is shorter.
Jill:	She sticks out just the same. Wait for Warren.
Fred:	Now she's longer than before, that's why.
Teacher:	Is there a way to measure the rug so we don't have to worry about people's sizes?
Kenny:	Use short people.
Teacher:	And if the short people aren't in school?
Rose:	Use big people.
Eddie:	Some people are too big.
Teacher:	Maybe using people is a problem.
Fred:	Use three-year-olds.
Teacher:	There aren't any three-year-olds in our class.
Deana:	Use rulers. Get all the rulers in the room. I'll get the box of rulers.
Eddie:	That was *my* idea, you know.
Deana:	This isn't enough rulers.
Eddie:	Put a short, short person after the rulers—Andy.
Andy:	I'm not short, short. And I'm not playing this game.
Wally:	Use the dolls.
Teacher:	So this rug is ten rulers and two dolls long? (*Silence*.) Here's something we can do. We can use one of the rulers over again, this way.

Eddie: Now you made *another* empty space.
Teacher: Eddie, you mentioned a tape measure
              before. I have one here.
*(We stretch the tape along the edge of the rug, and
I show the children that the rug is 156 inches long.
The lesson is done. The next day Warren is back in
school.)*
Wally: Here's Warren. Now we can really
              measure the rug.
Teacher: Didn't we really measure the rug with
              the ruler?
Wally: Well, rulers aren't really real, are
              they?

Rulers are not real, but rug measurers are. Dressing up to
look like a mother and using magic to become a lion is real,
but having parents die is not real. Does "real" mean that
which can be imagined and acted out? Does Wally *see*
himself as a mother lion rather than expect to *be* one? Wally
once told Eddie he was going to grow up and become
Superman. "You can't do that, Wally," Eddie said.
Whereupon Wally altered his statement to "I mean *look* like
Superman," and Eddie approved.

I discovered that the scale I had just paid twenty dollars for
was no more real than the tape measure. We were about to
act out *Stone Soup*, by Marcia Brown, a story about three
hungry soldiers who trick some selfish peasants into giving
them food by pretending to make soup out of three stones.
As part of the play, the children brought vegetables to cook.

"Do stones melt?" Rose suddenly asked. "Do we eat the
stones?"

"Do you think they melt, Rose?"

"Yes."

I looked around at serious faces. "Does anyone agree with
Rose?"

"They *will* melt if you cook them," said Lisa.

"If you *boil* them," Eddie added.

No one doubted that the stones in the story had melted and that ours too would melt.

"We can cook them and find out," I said. "How will we be able to tell if they've melted?"

"They'll be smaller," said Deana.

I lower three stones into boiling water. "How long shall they boil?" I ask. The suggestions range from a few minutes to ten hours. We decide on one hour and finish the story while the stones cook. Just before lunch we remove the stones and place them on a table.

Ellen: They're much smaller.

Fred: Much, much. Almost melted.

Rose: I can't eat melted stones.

Teacher: Don't worry, Rose. You won't. But I'm not convinced they've melted. Can we prove it?

Mickey: Draw a picture of them.

Teacher: And cook them again? All right.

(*Mickey and Earl trace the stones on a piece of paper, and I put them back in the water to cook some more. Thirty minutes later the stones do look smaller.*)

Teacher: I know they seem smaller, but it's very hard to match stones and patterns. Is there another way to prove whether the stones have melted?

(*There is no response. Clearly I am after the "right" answer, but the children have enough proof that the stones have melted.*)

Teacher: Let's weigh them on this scale. How much do they weigh?

Everyone: Two.
Teacher: Two pounds.
Lisa: Do we have to cook them again?
             They'll just keep melting.
Teacher: Maybe not.
(After a short period we weigh the stones again.)
Eddie: Still two. But they *are* smaller.
Wally: Much smaller.
Teacher: They weigh the same. Two pounds
             before and two pounds now. That
             means they didn't lose weight.
Eddie: They only got a *little* bit smaller.
Wally: The scale can't *see* the stones. Hey,
             once in Michigan there were three
             stones in a fire and they melted away.
             They were gone. We saw it.
Deana: Maybe the stones in the story are
             magic.
Wally: But not these.

The endless contradictions did not offend them; the children did not demand consistency. Once Lisa told us that she and her family did not believe in the tooth fairy. Her mother gave her a quarter for her tooth. I asked what her mother would do with the tooth and why it was worth a quarter to her. "She can sell it to the tooth fairy and get real gold for it." Lisa saw nothing inconsistent about combining both ideas.

Nor did anyone at Lisa's table think it strange when she asked me if I were really Mrs. Paley. I had spoken of Mr. Paley during lunch and Lisa was surprised. "Then are you really Mrs. Paley?"

"Lisa, you know that's my name," I said.

"Yes," she replied, "but I thought you just called yourself that."

Jealousy

Scales do not see what they measure, and teachers' names are merely labels, but melted stones and tooth fairies are believable. Was the time-out chair real to them—or did it measure behavior as mysteriously as the ruler measured the rug? Even worse, did my punishment carry a message of fairy-tale retribution rather than the sensible lesson I envisioned?

Shortly after we read "The Three Pigs," this conversation took place.

Andy:	There's a boy Jeffrey on the other block from me. I went to his house once and he wouldn't let me in.
Lisa:	Why?
Andy:	Someone else was there.
Wally:	You should have gone down the chimney.
Lisa:	You shouldn't sneak into someone's house.
Eddie:	He should shape his hair in a different way and then come back and Jeffrey'll say "Come in" and tell the other boy to go home.
Fred:	If he went down the chimney he might get boiled.

Wally: He could come down with a gun.
Eddie: Just to scare him. If he puts a boiling pot there, just jump over it.
Lisa: Not a gun.
Eddie: Here's a great idea. Get bullets and put it in the gun and aim it at Jeffrey.
Teacher: That's a great idea?
Eddie: No, I mean it's a bad idea.
Lisa: Well, let him come down the chimney but not with a gun.
Wally: Let's all go to Jeffrey's house and climb down his chimney and make him let Andy come in.
Andy: I'll find out if he has a chimney.
Wally: I'll get a time-out chimney and he has to stay in there until he lets you come in.

I was not surprised by Wally's fantasy solution to Andy's problem, because the image of not being allowed into the house recalled the chimney from "The Three Pigs." But his use of a time-out contrivance was interesting. In classroom conflicts, such as the following one in the record corner, the children did not seek to resolve the problem by isolating their classmates.

Jill: Every time I listen to the Ella Jenkins record, you know it's supposed to say "Yes ma'am," but Tanya says "No ma'am" louder and louder.
Tanya: So does Wally.
Wally: I only did it once.
Jill: Tanya *keeps keeps* doing it.
Teacher: You told her to stop?

Jill:	I *keep keep* telling her. The next time she comes in and I put on that record I'm going to just take it off.
Teacher:	Why do that? There should be a rule about bothering people when they're listening to records.
Jill:	Next time Tanya comes in I'm going to leave.
Teacher:	Why should you be the one to leave?
Jill:	So she won't bother me.
Deana:	Here's a good rule: if you want to fool around, don't sing with a record.
Wally:	Whoever says "No ma'am" has to say "Yes ma'am."
Mickey:	Keep changing the record until you find one Tanya likes.
Teacher:	Is that fair to Jill?
Mickey:	Sure. Jill could listen to the different record too.
Teacher:	Tanya, it seems to me *you* should leave if you spoil the record, but they don't agree with me.
Tanya:	If I do it again I'll just take a book until I stop saying "No ma'am."
Jill:	Or maybe I'll just put on a record you like.

The previous day I had made Tanya leave the art table after she splattered paint on Ellen's picture. Tanya shouted, "I'm never going to paint again!" After lunch she returned to the painting table and repeated her mischief. Lisa looked up and said, "Tanya's just jealous."

In the record corner the childen said: we like you, Tanya, and you can stay. They did not withhold friendship or impose hardships, and Tanya stopped teasing. I had excluded Tanya from the art table and achieved little besides temporary peace and quiet.

Left to themselves, the children recognized and attended to the real issue: jealousy. They seemed to judge social behavior by two sets of rules: acts that deliberately provoked jealousy were "no fair" and not excused; other conduct was tolerated.

Eddie:	My father brought me this from his trip. It's much bigger than my other Spiderman. This part moves.
Wally:	Hey, can I play with that?
Eddie:	Just wait.
Andy:	I'm next.
Eddie:	I can't give so many turns.
Andy:	You're not coming to my birthday.
Eddie:	Okay, you can be after Wally.
Fred:	I'm next after him then.
Eddie:	That's too many. My mother said only two people.
Fred:	Who cares! Don't play with him, Wally! (*He pushes the doll and starts to cry.*) C'mon, let's not be his friend. He has to put it away.
Eddie:	Oh yeah? You didn't that other time. That Superman doll? And I didn't get a turn.
Fred:	You did too!
Eddie:	Not so many turns.
Fred:	You're not supposed to bring it to school.
Eddie:	So what? Anyway, I changed my mind. I don't want to play with it. I'm not supposed to get it dirty anyway.

Eddie puts the doll in his cubby and the boys are instantly amiable. Later, however, Eddie breaks a clay house made by Earl. It is obvious he has done it on purpose.

Teacher: Why did you do that, Eddie? That was not nice!

Lisa: He has to make Earl another house.

Warren: Don't let him play with clay for two days.

Wally: Let him pick his own punishment. Okay, Eddie?

Eddie: I'm not picking a punishment and I don't care if I ever play with clay. And I didn't know it was Earl's house.

Teacher: Well, it had to be someone's house, didn't it?

Tanya: Let Eddie invite Earl to his house and Earl can decide everything they do all day long.

Fred: Let Earl break something of Eddie's.

Teacher: Which idea sounds fair, Earl?

Earl: That Eddie makes me a new house.

Eddie: I don't want to.

Wally: Okay. Let someone else do it.

Fred: I'll do it!

Earl: Fred can do it.

Teacher: How about Eddie?

Earl: He'll do it some other time.

Eddie's right to be difficult was respected, but not his right to bring the Spiderman doll. This view of the social contract was quite different from my own. I discriminated far less among different kinds of aggressive behavior; the child clearly defined "bad" as an action that made him jealous.

Wally:	Here's something really not fair. Deana and Jill always pick the very same people to act in their stories. They never pick me.
Teacher:	But they write the story. Can't they pick the actors?
Everyone:	No!
Ellen:	Then people just feel bad. You have to pick someone who didn't have a turn.
Wally:	I only got one turn. In my own story.
Deana:	I only got four turns.
Andy:	I *never* had a turn!
Tanya:	Yes, you did too. You were the lion in my story.
Wally:	He was a wolf. I was the lion.
Teacher:	How can we remember who had turns?
Deana:	Go cubby by cubby—like for leaders.
Wally:	Start with my cubby because I'm down by the door.
Deana:	Start with Rose because she never writes a story.
Wally:	Okay, start with Rose.

They worry about Rose, who never writes stories and therefore never gets first choice of roles. Tanya feels left out in the record corner, so they look for a record she will like. Eddie can make up for his transgressions at another time when he's in a better mood. Fairness is given a high priority in the kindergarten.

Fairness

These kindergarten children are finding out they can make significant, lasting changes in their own social organization, and they are certain that absolute safety lies in absolute fairness. It is a heady feeling, encouraging the most advanced thinking and speaking skills in the cause of establishing rules of fairness.

When we read stories, for example, the children pay close attention to the issue of justice. At such times my ideas about fairness may be as far from the children's as is my faith in the scale.

"There was a bird named Tico and he didn't have any friends because all his friends had black wings and they didn't like him anymore because he asked the wishingbird for golden wings."

Lisa is telling us the story of *Tico and the Golden Wings* by Leo Lionni. The children and I do not agree about Tico; I applaud him as a nonconformist while they see him as a threat to the community.

This is the story: Tico, a wingless bird, is cared for by his bird friends. One night a wishingbird grants Tico his wish for golden wings. This angers his black-winged peers who abandon him, saying, "You wanted to be different." Perplexed and hurt, Tico discovers he can exchange his golden feathers for black ones by performing good deeds. When at last his wings are black, Tico is welcomed back to the flock, who observe, "Now you are just like us."

> *Teacher*:   I don't think it's fair that Tico has
> to give up his golden wings.

Lisa:	It *is* fair. See, he was nicer when he didn't have any wings. They didn't like him when he had gold.
Wally:	He thinks he's better if he has golden wings.
Eddie:	He *is* better.
Jill:	But he's not supposed to be better. The wishingbird was wrong to give him those wings.
Deana:	She *has* to give him his wish. He's the one who shouldn't have asked for golden wings.
Wally:	He could put black wings on top of the golden wings and try to trick them.
Deana:	They'd sneak up and see the gold. He should just give every bird one golden feather and keep one for himself.
Teacher:	Why can't he decide for himself what kind of wings he wants?
Wally:	He *has* to decide to have black wings.

The author upholds the peer-group point of view. It is the same judgment Eddie received when he displayed his new giant Spiderman doll: do not make your friends jealous.

But what happens when your friends make you jealous? There is a story for this too, and again I support the opposite side. In the story, a Japanese folktale called *A Blue Seed* by Rieko Nakagawa, a fox gives a little boy a blue seed in exchange for a toy airplane. The seed sprouts a tiny blue house, which grows bigger and bigger as a happy group of animals and children join the boy in the house. Suddenly the fox returns, demands the house, and orders everyone out.

Whereupon the house increases in size until it reaches the sun
and explodes.

> *Teacher*: Was it fair for the fox to chase every-
>   one out of the house?
> *Eddie*:   He wanted the seed back.
> *Deana*:   He needed his own house back. Maybe
>   he never had his own house.
>   Maybe he always had to share.
> *Ellen*:   He shouldn't have traded the blue
>   seed.
> *Wally*:   But he didn't know it was going to
>   grow into a house. See, the house
>   wanted to be shared but it really
>   belonged to the fox because it was
>   his seed and he didn't have to share
>   it if he wanted it for himself.
> *Eddie*:   Wally's right. Those other people
>   had their own house. They didn't
>   need to live in the fox's house.

No wonder punishment doesn't work. I would have
punished the fox, and the children think the fox is right. I
defend Tico, but the children say Tico is wrong. Now I
understand why Wally has to ask me every day if he is good.
Our definitions of goodness do not always match.

A week later Wally dictates a new script for Tico.

There was a bird named Tico and his fairy god-
mother said, "I'll give you golden wings if you kill
the giant." And then he waited until the giant was
sleeping and then he chopped off his head and then

he took the chicken that laid golden eggs and then
the fairy gave him golden wings.

"This is a different Tico story," Wally says as I write down
his words. "When can we act it out? I'll be Tico."

"We can do it now, but first I have a question, Wally. How
about Tico's friends? Do they fly away when they see his
golden wings?"

"Of course not! His wish *has* to come true. He killed the
giant!"

Wally has transformed Tico into a hero who is no longer at
the mercy of the group's mundane demands. Tico has
performed a daring feat and can keep the prize.

When we acted the original story, Wally did not want to
be Tico, preferring instead to be one of the bossy friends.
Now that Tico is a hero, Wally will play the role. The bird
friends don't even get a part—fantasies do not have to be
democratic.

Magic

Families were often the subject of Wally's stories; he explored
various combinations and possibilities in family life. His own
family consisted of his mother, his grandmother, and
himself, but his stories included fathers, brothers, sisters, and
lions.

Once upon a time a man went out to hunt and his
son went with him. He found a lion and the lion

killed the boy but the man had two sons and one
was still at home. So he shot the lion and he and
the other brother ate it for supper and then they
went to bed.

Wally's lions were usually aggressive beasts, but in one
story he turned a girl lion into a sister.

Once there was a boy hunter. His little sister didn't
like him so he ran away. So he found a baby girl
lion. Then he found a girl. "You can both be my
sisters," he said. Then they met a good fairy and
she turned the girl lion into a girl person so he had
two real sisters. They lived happily ever after.

"Wally," I asked, "could the girl lion really turn into a girl
person?"

"If God wanted that. First He finds out if the girl lion wants
to become a girl person and then He tells a fairy to do it
because He's busy."

"Could a magician do it?"

"God likes fairies better."

The real power then is in the wish. Even a girl lion is given
the option to remain herself if she wishes. God must observe
the rules by which wishes are carried out, and it is the
children who invent the rules. If fairness insures safety in the
present, wishing guarantees it for the future.

Magic weaves in and out of everything the children say
and do. The boundaries between what the child thinks and
what the adult sees are never clear to the adult, but the child
does not expect compatibility. The child himself is the
ultimate magician. He credits God and lesser powers, but it is

the child who confirms the probability of events. If he can imagine something, it exists.

Wally:	I know all about Jonas. He got swallowed by the whale.
Fred:	How?
Wally:	God sent him. But the whale was asleep so he just walked out.
Fred:	How did he fly up to God? I mean how did he get back to shore if it was so deep?
Wally:	He didn't come from the sky. But he could have because there's an ocean in the sky. For the rain to come down.
Fred:	Oh yeah. That's for the gods. When they go deep they never drown, do they?
Wally:	Of course not. They're just going nearer to Earth.
Jill:	How does the ocean stay up?
Fred:	They patch it up. They . . .
Wally:	They take a big, big, big bag and put it around the ocean.
Fred:	It's a very, very, very big bag.
Eddie:	Which reminds me. Do you know how many Christmas trees God gets? Infinity.
Teacher:	Who gives Him Christmas trees?
Eddie:	He makes them.
Wally:	When people burn them . . . You see He's invisible. He takes up the burned parts and puts them together.

Rose:	Are there decorations?
Wally:	Invisible decorations. He can see them because He's invisible. If you tell Him there's an invisible person here, He believes it.
Eddie:	You can't fool God.
Wally:	Sure you can. It's a good trick. You can say, "I'm here," and you're really not, but He can't see you. He can only see invisible things. You can fool Him.
Eddie:	But He hears you.
Wally:	Right. He hears you talk. He talks, too. But you have to ask Him. He talks very soft. I heard Him.
Eddie:	You know, 353 years ago everyone could see God. He wasn't invisible then. He was young so He could stay down on Earth. He's so old now He floats up in the sky. He lived in Uganda and Egypt.
Fred:	That's good, because everyone in Egypt keeps. They turn into mummies.

How does the child think of such things, the adult wonders. The child reasons that if a big bag in the sky or invisible decorations on heavenly Christmas trees were not possible, he could not have thought of them. As soon as he learns a language well enough, and *before* he is told he cannot invent the world, he will explain everything. This ability to imagine the beginnings and ends of events is most highly developed during the kindergarten year.

Wishes

The librarian told the children that if they listened quietly to her story they could make a wish that would come true "in a year and a day." Her promise bothered me. I felt the children were being tricked into good behavior. I brought up the subject with the children later in the day.

Teacher:	I've never heard of making a wish after a fairy tale. I'm not sure I agree with the librarian.
Eddie:	It could happen, because I lost a gorilla from my adventure set and I wished for it and I found it.
Jill:	Wishes do come true, you know.
Teacher:	But how does the librarian know they'll come true in a year and a day?
Wally:	See, one day *she* made a wish after listening quietly to a story and it came true in a year and a day.
Andy:	I made a wish that my daddy would bring me a toy from downtown and he did it in *one* day.
Teacher:	What causes wishes to come true?
Jill:	Just by themselves. Or they're not wishes.
Deana:	Fairies do it. It *has* to be fairies. I lost my library book and I wished I would find it and it came true in two days. That's because it was an *easy* wish.

Wally:	If the fairy is busy with teeth, Santa Claus might do it.
Teacher:	Could someone tell us what he wished for in the library?
Everyone:	You're not supposed to tell!
Teacher:	Why not?
Andy:	She said so!
Teacher:	How does she know?
Lisa:	It's really true. Once I wished for something and I told someone and it didn't come true.
Teacher:	What if I wished for six new slides for the playground?
Lisa:	That's too much. You can't wish for that much.
Andy:	Sure you can. But then you have to wait a long time.
Fred:	Can you wish for a mountain? No, you can't.
Wally:	Yes, you can. But not on top of the school because then it would smash up the school.
Lisa:	A mountain is too high to wish for.
Wally:	I wished for a mountain and in a year and a day there was a mountain. But not in Chicago.
Lisa:	Oh, you mean where there's room for mountains.

Children do not believe everything an adult says, but they believe opinions that support the legitimacy of magic. Questions concerning the circumstances in which wishes may be made are taken seriously.

Teacher: Has anyone seen the little blue racing
             car? The one with number 2 on it?
Andy: You could wish for it after the
             librarian's story.
Teacher: I think I'm better off searching for
             it, Andy.
Wally: You're better off wishing. Then you
             don't have to search. If you make a
             wish, don't search. Wait for the fairy
             to do it.
Teacher: Well, I could wish for it every day
             when I come to school.
Eddie: That's too much. Every day is too
             much.
Wally: Right. God gets tired of so many
             wishes. Then He might decide not to
             give you your wish.
Deana: The fairies get tired too. Just make
             one tiny, quiet wish. Just one.

Fairies, then, and perhaps even God, react in the manner
of parents and teachers. Pestering can be counterproductive;
make your wish and wait patiently. Wishing too often or for
too much is foolish. In the world of fairies, greed and
impatience are not tolerated.

Teacher: Where do you children get all
             these ideas about wishing?
Andy: From God. He makes up everything.
Wally: First God thinks it up to Himself
             and then He puts it into your mind.

Eddie: But some ideas come from your
              mother and father.
Wally: *After* God puts it into their mind.
Deana: I think it just comes from your
              mind. Your mind tells you what to
              think.
Eddie: Here's how it happens:
              You remember things other people say
              and you see everything, and then your
              mind gives you spaces to keep all the
              rememberings and then you say it.
Wally: Don't forget, Eddie, that God makes
              you remember. He tells you if it's
              a good idea.
Lisa: Maybe it's a bad idea.
Wally: He tells bad people bad things.
Teacher: Why is that?
Wally: So the good people can tell the bad
              people to be good.
Teacher: How do people get thoughts about
              things they've never seen or heard?
Andy: In dreams.
Eddie: In bad dreams. They scare you and
              then you remember them.
Fred: You could make up dreams.
Andy: I'm pretty sure dreams come from God.
Fred: Maybe your mind is invisible when
              you sleep.
Eddie: Oh, then that's how. God is invisible
              too. He sees anything invisible so He
              can see your dreams.
Teacher: Does God want to scare you with bad
              dreams?
Eddie: He would *never* do that. That's why
              he wakes you up.

Children insist that God behaves sensibly. They envision an orderly world in which there are answers for every question and few limits are imposed on the imagination. However, they all agree on the roles played by God and the fairies: they bring harmony out of discordant notes.

One day we soaked beans to prepare them for planting. When Rose looked at the shriveled cover of her bean she shuddered. "That scares me when the skin comes off."

Lisa understood her problem. "Don't worry, Rose. The bean fairy wants your bean to have a new dress."

Surely no adult could have made Rose feel so protected at that moment. Did Lisa believe in a bean fairy? It would be fair to say that having thought of a bean fairy, she knew what a bean fairy would do to comfort Rose.

Wally needed comfort from fairies, too. Sometimes, when his own story saddened him, he would bring in a fairy to set things right.

> Once upon a time there was a father and he had four boys. One of them went out to see the woods and a lion killed him. He didn't come back for four days and then the father went out to find him. The father broke his arm and two of the sons carried him back. They took the father to the hospital. He couldn't come home for a year. The last day he died. Then the two boys went back to the forest and a fairy said the other brother was still alive because he was only resting and he just looked dead. So they all lived happily ever after.

Fairies

"Why did God invent checkers so you can't move backwards?" Eddie wondered. He was losing in our game of checkers.

"Did God invent checkers?" I asked.

"It had to be God because a magician would trick you," Eddie replied. "By the way," he said a few moments later, "Warren moves on the red spaces."

"Why didn't you show him how to play?"

"I did, but he keeps doing it. I think it's because he's Chinese."

"I doubt if Chinese people play checkers in a different way, Eddie."

"Sure they do. God invented a different way to play in Chinese. What's the use of being Chinese if you don't do things different?"

Children provide their Magical Beings with a continual supply of reasonable answers and specific expectations. God represents order and fairness; everything that depends on rules is attributed to Him. Fairies are likely to be associated with the pleasant surprises in life, magicians with tricks and mischief. Fairies, being more like God, can be trusted; magicians are more like people and must be viewed cautiously.

No fairy is heralded more than the tooth fairy, and the kindergarten is her kingdom. The first tooth loss usually occurs between five and six, and the idea of being rewarded by a fairy suits the child's notion of the kind of world God runs.

Although Wally had been tempted to trick God, he would not consider tricking the tooth fairy. When Kim told him her cousin fooled the tooth fairy by placing a kernel of corn under her pillow, he was incensed.

"I don't believe you! You're lying!" We were coming back from a farm trip shortly before Halloween, and Kim had been staring at the bushel of corn next to her feet. Wally sat beside her on the bus seat, holding a big pumpkin on his lap.

"It's true. Ask my mother. She believes my cousin." When challenged, one could always call on an absent mother for verification.

I leaned over from across the aisle. "I heard you arguing about the tooth fairy. Do you mind if I ask the other children for their opinions tomorrow?"

Wally answered quickly. "Sure. That'll be a good discussion for you."

Table 1

Teacher:	Wally said you can't fool the tooth fairy. Kim thinks you might trick her with a piece of corn.
Jill:	He's right. You shouldn't try because she wouldn't trick *you*. Only magicians trick people.
Deana:	Magicians can make things disappear.
Lisa:	So can fairies.
Wally:	Magicians make things invisible and fairies don't.
Eddie:	Wait a minute, Wally! You forgot something. Magicians can't make *themselves* invisible and fairies can become invisible any time they want to.

Wally:	Oh, yeah. Else how could they take your tooth?

Table 2

Teacher:	Wally told Kim that nobody can fool the tooth fairy. Kim thinks you might be able to do it.
Warren:	She could be in your room waiting until you fall asleep. Or she could come through the door.
Tanya:	Not in my house. My daddy, he double locks all the doors and windows. No one can have a key to the back door unless my daddy says so.
Warren:	The tooth fairy comes through the wall. But a magician can trick people like this: he puts on a disguise and then he says, "Here's some new keys. The old ones don't fit." Then he keeps a key for himself so he can sneak in.
Tanya:	He can't fool my daddy.
Warren:	He can't fool God but he can always fool people.
Mickey:	Unless God tells you the magic words.
Andy:	Like in church?
Tanya:	Oh, that's how? My daddy knows about that. That's praying. I didn't know that was magic words.

Table 3

Teacher:	Kim said she might try to fool the tooth fairy.
Ellen:	How would she do that?
Teacher:	By pretending a kernel of corn was a tooth.

Ellen:	She couldn't do that. You have to have a place in your mouth for the tooth.
Rose:	Can she see the space if your mouth is closed?
Ellen:	She's invisible. She can see inside your mouth.
Tanya:	Here's how you could trick her. When your tooth comes out put the corn in the envelope. Then she'll give you a quarter. Then in two nights put the tooth in the envelope. Then you'll get another quarter.
Earl:	She'll smell the corn. Teeth don't smell that way.

Table 4

Teacher:	Kim, do you still think you can fool the tooth fairy?
Kim:	My sister says there isn't even a tooth fairy. She says it's our mother.
Teacher:	What do you think?
Kim:	I think the fairy came in after my sister was asleep. Because my sister said I would get one dime and I got two dimes.
Kenny:	I got a dollar. My mom can't spend a dollar because we're saving money for a car. So it has to be the tooth fairy.
Teacher:	Can you trick her?
Kenny:	A magician can trick her.
Teacher:	Who knows more magic, fairies or magicians?

Kim:	Fairies make things come true.
	Magicians just do magical things.
Teacher:	The magical things aren't true?
Kim:	They just pretend it's true.
Teacher:	Is God a magician?
Everyone:	Oh no! Of course not!
Kenny:	He made the whole world. Then he
	went up to the sky to live so he could
	watch everyone.

Over the years there have been many variations on the tooth fairy but little doubt of her existence. In each class there are always two or three children who insist they have seen her. No one challenges these stories, for the children want proof of the existence of fairies.

⌐ Begin

Wally:	The tooth fairy came in my room and
	woke me up.
Teacher:	What did she look like?
Wally:	She was pretty and had long hair.
Teacher:	Was she old?
Wally:	Not as old as a grand person.
	As old as you. She put an envelope
	with money under my pillow.
Teacher:	Tanya says the tooth fairy can't get
	into her house. Her daddy locks all
	the doors and windows.
Warren:	She flies through the glass.
Wally:	No, she comes in through the roof.
Teacher:	Where does she get all the money?
Wally:	From the bank.

Deana:	He's right. I *saw* her at the bank. She had purple shoes and red hair.
Andy:	Did she talk to you?
Deana:	She doesn't speak English. I think she talks in Chinese.
Eddie:	Does she, Warren?
Warren:	Probably she does.

Akemi, from Japan, and Ramsi, from Iraq, had not heard of the tooth fairy. I invited Ramsi's mother to visit us and explain what happens in Iraq when a child loses a tooth. She told us that tooth fairies are not found in Moslem countries.

"Our custom is rather nice, though. The child throws the tooth toward the sun and says in Arabic, 'Oh sun, take this donkey's tooth and give me a gazelle's tooth.' Sometimes they say, 'Take this bad tooth and give me a good tooth.' "

"Then the fairy comes?" asked Rose.

"I'll ask Ramsi what he thinks," said his mother. Ramsi looked around shyly and then said, "It could be a fairy."

"Will the fairy leave Ramsi a dime?" asked Deana.

"I think that is probably what will happen," Ramsi's mother replied.

I asked a psychiatrist friend if there was any specific trauma associated with the loss of a tooth.

"If you mean, is it akin to castration feelings, I don't think so, though many of my colleagues might disagree with me," he replied. "It's a minor discomfort for the young child and, with adequate preparation, can be handled without difficulty. As soon as the first permanent tooth appears, the mystery is over. We mistakenly feel we must compensate our children for this loss whereas the real compensation is the new tooth as a symbol of maturity."

My friend sounded authoritative, but I decided to ask the children.

Teacher:	Should a child receive money for a tooth? After all, a new tooth comes in very soon.
Eddie:	But the tooth fairy wants to give you a present. Because she has your tooth.
Teacher:	Why does she want all those teeth?
Wally:	She gives them to the little babies. They're baby teeth.

Kindergarten children are experts on the tooth fairy. Adult stories cannot compete with the inventions of five-year-olds. I brought the matter to Wally's attention one day when he and I went to get the milk.

"We read so many good fairy tales, Wally, but none are about tooth fairies. I wonder why?"

"They write in invisible ink," he answered, "so no one knows where they hide the money. Or the teeth."

Halloween would soon be here and the talk was not of fairies, but rather of candy and costumes. When Tanya mentioned her family custom of making a wish on a pumpkin, nearly everyone opposed the idea.

Tanya:	In my house we make a wish when we blow out the candle in the pumpkin.
Lisa:	You're making that up.
Tanya:	No I'm not. Ask my mother.
Wally:	You can't wish on a pumpkin. It's not a magic thing.

Teacher:	Are teeth magic?
Wally:	They don't have to be. They belong to the tooth fairy.
Teacher:	Maybe pumpkins belong to the pumpkin fairy.
Lisa:	There's no pumpkin fairy.
Teacher:	Why not?
Eddie:	You just ring the bell and everybody gives you candy. Even if you don't ask. Fairies are for wishes.
Tanya:	My brother said the witches can steal your candy.
Eddie:	There's no real witches on Halloween. That's a lie. They just put on costumes. They go to a store and get a broom.
Deana:	Real witches are only in stories.

The children were cautious. Witches are too dangerous to be allowed out of the fairy tale; they must be controlled. If the magician is the undependable and unpredictable adult, the witch embodies the child's worst fears.

Teacher:	I wonder why people talk about a tooth fairy and not a tooth witch?
Jill:	A tooth fairy comes through the wall and a witch has to knock on the door.
Wally:	If a witch came he might steal the child away.
Eddie:	Jill, I don't think a witch would knock—she'll break the door open. She could even steal a mother away.
Jill:	The tooth fairy would leave a quarter and then the witch comes and steals the money. But then you wish for it again.

Warren: A witch could take the pillow away. Wait, first she puts her magic stick under the pillow, then she makes the pillow disappear, then the stick hurts your head. Then your mother has to come in and sleep with you because you might be bleeding.

Deana: Tooth witches would leave spiders on the money.

Kim: There's no such thing as a tooth witch.

Deana: I know. I mean if there was.

Kim: Witches can't be invisible. So only a fairy can be a tooth fairy.

Deana: Fairies are always good. If they do something bad they can become a witch. Then, in six hundred years, a witch can be a fairy again.

Wally: Oh, so that's how they have good witches in *The Wizard of Oz*.

Deana neatly handled the troubling concept of the good witch; it is a matter of faith buttressed by necessity. A good witch is a contradiction in terms, but six hundred years is distant enough to appear safe.

The issue of personal safety makes children quite exacting in their rules for invisible phenomena. Only invisible beings can see things that are invisible. One must make certain that potentially harmful occurrences are seen and controlled by the right people, so magicians and witches are seldom permitted to become invisible.

Wally had to revise one story because of an invisible witch. This was his original story.

Once there was a little boy and he went out of the house and then the father got home. The father didn't see him so he went out to find the boy. Then the father saw a lion. He started to shoot but the lion became invisible because it was really an invisible witch. Then the witch killed the father and the boy went home and he lived with his mother and sister.

Kim objected. "I don't want that part!" It was her turn, according to the list of names we now followed, but she refused to be the lion who becomes an invisible witch. "I'll only be a good witch."

"Okay, okay. I'll change it," said Wally. "The lion becomes invisible because it was really the pet lion of a good witch and she didn't want it to get killed. So the father found the boy and they killed a giraffe and ate it for their dinner."

Rose

"Are you sad, Wally?" Rose was bending over Wally, their faces almost touching.

"I'm just thinking."

"What're you thinking about?"

"About sad things."

Rose sat next to him. Her face said she meant to think about sad things too. Rose was like the sister in Wally's stories—the one the little brother lives with happily ever after. She was there to care about Wally.

Wally returned this love in a specific way: he was Rose's teacher. Rose watched Wally's moods, but Wally listened to Rose's words. To be exact, Wally examined what was *wrong* with Rose's words. Too often, Rose did not "make sense." Her reasoning could be hard to follow, and she lacked the flexibility to clarify her statements.

Lisa:	(*Pouring tea.*) My daddy says black people come from Africa.
Wally:	I come from Chicago.
Lisa:	White people are born in America.
Wally:	I'm black and I was born in Chicago.
Rose:	Because more people come dressed up like they want to.
Wally:	How do they dress up?
Rose:	You know, like going to church or someplace.
Wally:	You mean if they're black?
Rose:	They can dress up like they want to.
Wally:	I see what she means. Like getting dressed up to go to church?
Rose:	Like they want to.
Wally:	Not in a black dress, right? You can wear a white dress?
Rose:	Yes.

These were the times when Rose, so sensitive to people, did not seem to listen to her own words; her phrases were mismatched, out of joint.

Rose:	Sometimes my other school is better than this school is better.

Teacher:	Your other school was better?
Rose:	This school is better than my other school is better.
Teacher:	Rose, do you like both schools the same?
Rose:	No.
Teacher:	Did you like your old school better than this school?
Rose:	Just the other one.
Teacher:	That was the one Wally went to, right? Remember you told me about Wally getting a spanking?
Rose:	Wally wasn't with Marie.
Teacher:	Did he have a different teacher?
Rose:	Just the other one.

Perhaps Rose finds it hard to talk of her day-care experience, I thought. Wally's unfavored position must have worried her. However, the following conversation between Rose and Lisa dealt with a simple point.

"What do you do with milk, Lisa?"

"What do you mean?" Lisa responded. "Drink it?"

"Oh, Lisa, you don't mean it," laughed Rose.

"Do you mean put it on cereal?"

"No, *what* do you do with milk? *What?*"

"I don't know that riddle," said Lisa.

"Never mind," said Rose, disappointed.

A few moments later I asked Rose, "What do *you* do with milk, Rose?"

"I don't know," she answered, which was to say, let me be. She looked trapped, as though she were about to be caught in a mistake.

Most children have learned a language and do make sense

by the time they enter kindergarten. Even when, as in Wally's case, they reach the conclusion that a boy can become a mother lion, their words and reasoning are clear. Wally believed in magic; every word explained his idea. An adult who agreed with his premise might use the same words.

Rose, however, was not convinced that words had commonly accepted meanings; she did not always make the connections between words and the actions that followed. After several hearings of *The Five Chinese Brothers*, in which one brother "swallows the sea," we discovered while acting the story that Rose heard "sea" as "seed." The picture in the book shows a man kneeling on a beach, drinking the sea. His cheeks fill until his head is huge with water. Soon the sea bed is emptied and only shells and fish are visible. Then, unable to contain the sea any longer, he expels it forcefully, and his head returns to its original size.

Rose observed the pictures as she heard the words. She did not ask herself: how could the swallowing of a seed produce such an effect? For her, words and pictures did not have to be connected. She accepted confusion as a normal state. She didn't know she had a right to understand. However, acting out a story is a precise enterprise. When Rose put a bead on the rug and pretended to swallow it, the children asked what she was doing.

"I'm eating the seed, that's what," she said. Eddie saw the error first. "No, that's for planting. This is water. You know, a sea."

Rose was perplexed. Seeing that she had made a mistake, she stopped listening.

Wally took the bead out of her hand. "Pretend a fairy changed the seed into a big ocean. They call that a sea sometimes and sometimes they call it a ocean. Now just drink it up like the man in the book. Blow up your cheeks like this. Then blow it out like this way." Rose copied every motion Wally made and then did it by herself, grinning at him.

I would not have "explained" the difference between "sea" and "seed" by magically turning a seed into the sea. Yet why not? Wally's magic released Rose from her fear and embarrassment. Now she could listen and understand. When Rose had been repelled by the lima bean cover, Lisa's bean fairy had accomplished a similar result. I had been charmed by the bean fairy story but had not absorbed the lesson. Wally used the word "pretend" as a teaching tool. Although Lisa had not said "pretend," it was implied: pretend the shriveled-up skin of the bean is an old dress and a fairy is giving the bean a new dress. With this idea in mind, Rose had picked up the bean and stuck it in the dirt.

One day Rose began telling a Cinderella story. "Cinderella made her stepsisters," she dictated as I wrote the words.

"Made them what?" I asked.

"Made her stepsisters."

"Made them what?" What did she make them?"

"She *made* her stepsisters."

I called Deana over to our table. "Listen to Rose's story, would you? 'Cinderella made her stepsisters.' What do you think that means?"

Deana looked at the picture Rose had drawn. "Made them with a wand. There's the wand."

"I'm sorry, Rose. I didn't understand. Could you and Deana act it out and show me how it's done?"

Rose brought a stick from the wood box and told Deana to lie down. "When I touch you with the magic stick you have to jump up."

"Why does Cinderella have to *make* the sisters?" I asked. "Weren't they already alive, living with the stepmother?"

"My story is about a magic Cinderella. She makes them into *good* sisters."

I suddenly remembered the conversation at Rose's table when they were considering the possibility of fooling the tooth fairy. Rose had asked, "Can the tooth fairy see the empty space if your mouth is closed?"

It was a good question, one that anyone in the class might have asked. When Ellen reminded Rose that the tooth fairy was invisible, Rose understood immediately: the inside of your mouth is invisible and therefore can only be seen by someone who is also invisible. Later, when I heard Rose explain it all to Wally, he had no problem understanding her; her words accurately represented her thought.

We acted out Rose's story, her first, after lunch.

> Cinderella made her stepsisters. She was magic. Then they went outside to play. Then they met their fairy grandmother. Then Cinderella made the prince.

"Made him what?" asked Wally.
"To be her brother."

Bad and Good

Lisa wanted us to talk about a picture in her Abraham Lincoln book. Young Abe is seated in a one-room schoolhouse with a dozen other children while the schoolmaster brandishes a stick over them.

Lisa:	He hits you if you don't know the words.
Teacher:	Does this make the children learn the words?
Lisa:	It does. Because then when you get spanked you'll try to think harder.
Eddie:	Yeah, but what if people start jumping around the room because it hurts so much?
Tanya:	It'll still make them good. Because they keep getting a hit every day with the stick and so they do what the teacher says.
Lisa:	If the teacher is angry she'll hit them because they're not listening very good.
Teacher:	Lisa, I doubt if children listen better when they're hit.
Ellen:	They'll just waste time crying.
Eddie:	They could get angry and scribble or tear the book.
Lisa:	They won't do that because he might hit them again.
Eddie:	If you get hit with a stick you might grab the stick and hit the teacher.
Wally:	He'll just hit you harder. Anyway it's really a good thing because if he hits you then you know your answer

	is wrong so you try to think of the right answer.
Teacher:	But no one here is hit, and all of you give good answers in our discussions.
Wally:	In first grade you have to work harder so the teacher might have to hit you.
Teacher:	Not in this school, Wally. None of the teachers hit anyone.
Tanya:	The children *pretend* you're spanking them.
Teacher:	You *pretend* I'm spanking you?
Tanya:	They know they'll get a spanking if they're bad.
Teacher:	Even though no one ever has?
Lisa:	But they think they will. See, they have this certain idea in their mind.
Wally:	That teacher is just trying to make them good. That's the reason for the stick.
Teacher:	Remember when you got spanked, Wally, at your other school? Did it make you behave better or did it make you angry?
Wally:	Every time I got spanked I behaved good.
Teacher:	Well, even so, there must be another reason for being good because I don't spank you and still you all try to behave your best.
Lisa:	Maybe you'll give us candy if we're good.
Teacher:	Except that I don't give you candy.
Lisa:	You might change your mind.

The "spare the rod and spoil the child" philosophy appealed to Lisa, Wally, and Tanya, yet it was their behavior that improved the most *without* the rod. The children had vivid memories of bad feelings associated with adult anger, but they accepted that anger and punishment as a necessary part of life.

Eddie: Sometimes I hate myself.
Teacher: When?
Eddie: When I'm naughty.
Teacher: What do you do
             that's naughty?
Eddie: You know, naughty words. Like
             "shit." That one.
Teacher: That makes you hate yourself?
Eddie: Yeah, when my dad washes my mouth
             with soap.
Teacher: What if he doesn't hear you?
Eddie: Then I get away with it. Then I
             don't hate myself.
Wally: If I'm bad, like take the food when
             it's not time to eat yet and my mom
             makes me leave the kitchen, then I
             hate myself because I want to stay
             with her in the kitchen.
Eddie: And here's another reason when I
             don't like myself. This is a good
             reason. Sometimes I try to get the
             cookies on top of the refrigerator.
Teacher: What's the reason you don't like
             yourself?
Eddie: Because my mom counts to ten fast
             and I get a spanking and my grandma
             gets mad at her.

Deana: Here's when I *like* myself: when I'm
coloring and my mommy says, "Stop
coloring. We have to go out." And
I tell her I'm coloring and she says
"Okay, I'll give you ten more minutes."

Teacher: What if you have to stop what you're
doing?

Deana: When she's in a big hurry. That's
when she yells at me. Then I don't
like myself.

Bad and good depended on the adult response. If the
schoolteacher used a hickory stick, it meant that the children
were bad; the stick made them good. An angry parent
denoted a naughty child. To the adult, the cause of the
punishment was obvious, but the child saw only the stick and
judged himself accordingly.

Wally: In my old school, if you tore someone's
picture you sat in the hallway all alone
by yourself until you were good.

Teacher: Did it make you good?

Wally: Yes. Hey, you know what we did in
the hallway? We tore off the pictures
on the wall.

Teacher: Then being out in the hallway didn't
seem to make you good, did it?

Wally: They didn't know it was us.

Robbers

In the five-year-old's vision I was someone who just called myself Mrs. Paley. During our second attempt to grow lima beans, another aspect of my reality was discussed.

Teacher: Yesterday you said the beans didn't come up because we soaked them too long. The directions said "overnight," and we began to soak them in the morning. But how can we follow these directions if we all leave school in the afternoon?

Fred: Why can't you come back in the night?

Teacher: I suppose I could. But I'm busy at home making dinner and eating with my family.

Fred: Bring the food and fix it in the classroom. You could bring your family.

Lisa: Or you can soak the beans at your house.

Kenny: They'll spill if she does that.

Wally: Put on a cover.

Tanya: Stay at school to have a conference.

Teacher: My conferences are finished.

Kim: That's no fair if you take them home.

Teacher: I would bring them back the next day.

Kim: You should stay here with them.

Teacher: But my family will be waiting for me.

Wally: You can go home and get all the things you have to do and come back to school. Then when it gets dark,

	start soaking the beans. Then you can go back to your house again.
Teacher:	Yes, I could do that. But what's easier—to bring everything to school or to take the beans home?
All:	To take the beans home.
Teacher:	Then that's what I'll do.

The children preferred not to think of me or the beans in another place. I had soaked the beans in the classroom and that is where the beans—and I—belonged. The children could not envision my life away from school and had difficulty coordinating events in the classroom with those in my house.

Nor could they imagine the life of a bean. Neither life was a part of their personal knowledge, and they lacked the experience to improvise realistic solutions. The beans, planted in individual milk cartons, were watched, poked, and watered, all excessively. After three weeks only two green sprouts could be seen. Wally was the first to discover the disappearance of his beans.

"They're gone!" he yelled, bringing me his carton. "Gone! I looked through the whole dirt!"

"Can I look in mine?" asked Rose.

"You might as well," I answered. "They don't seem to be coming up."

There was a rush to the planting table. Everyone began digging into cartons or dumping their contents on the newspaper-covered table.

Andy:	Where are the beans?
Wally:	They're invisible.

Andy:	Impossible. They came from a store. Someone took them out.
Teacher:	Who?
Andy:	A robber.
Eddie:	When it was dark a criminal took them.
Teacher:	Why would he do it?
Jill:	Maybe someone came in and said, "Oh, there's nothing growing. We must take some of them out."
Eddie:	I think a robber broke in and said, "They don't need to plant those beans."
Teacher:	Why would a robber want them?
Wally:	To sell them.
Andy:	Or cook them.
Ellen:	No, maybe to fool people with. See, he could plant them in his garden and when flowers came up people would think he's nice.
Teacher:	If I were a robber I'd take the record player.
Eddie:	Not if you wanted to plant seeds.

The burglar's needs were not considered, any more than my out-of-classroom life had been. The children discounted the idea that the beans were invisible until Eddie brought an adult answer from home, then magic was considered.

"I told my dad about the beans," Eddie said the moment he walked in the next day. "He told me they dissolved just like sugar dissolves in coffee."

Warren and Wally were making snakes at the clay table. "Maybe a worm made them dissolve," Warren commented.

"Or something disguised as a worm," Wally completed the thought.

"What could be disguised as a worm?" I asked.

"You know, like if a magician was outside the window," Eddie answered. I wanted to ask him about his father's example of sugar dissolving in coffee, but I knew without asking. Children resist facts about unseen phenomena. Such facts are too hard to imagine and sometimes disturbing. Besides, magic gives explanatory power in a world where the adults seem to know everything.

A few days later I noticed a moldy, rotting pumpkin in another kindergarten room. I was told that the class was observing the gradual decay of its Halloween pumpkin. I asked if I could discuss the subject with them.

Teacher:	Why does your pumpkin look like this?
Tim:	It's full of mold.
Carter:	It's moldy. Plants are growing inside.
Julia:	Little vines.
William:	They make the top fall in.
Kevin:	Dead plants and animals get mold.
Tim:	Old pumpkins get moldy.
Julia:	It's going to become dust.
Teacher:	How does that happen?
Julia:	It'll get so dry you won't even see it.
Teacher:	By the way, we have a problem in our class. We planted lima beans and after a long time nothing came up. We looked in the dirt to see if any roots had grown and we couldn't find the beans. They were gone.
Kevin:	Was the window open? The wind blew them away.
Teacher:	They were deep down in the dirt.
Candy:	A squirrel could have took them.

Teacher:	We didn't see a squirrel in the room.
Candy:	It could have hid somewhere.
Teacher:	Our windows are locked at night. How could the squirrel have gotten back out?
William:	He could scratch a hole in the window.
Kevin:	Or in the door.
Carter:	Maybe a robber stepped in. They can get in windows very easily.
Teacher:	Why would he want the beans?
Carter:	For his garden.
Julia:	Or to cook them. Somebody has a key to your window, I think.

There was no further talk of squirrels once the robber theory was suggested. I was so surprised by this change of opinion after talking about a rotting pumpkin that I presented my question to the third kindergarten. One child said a bird might be the culprit, another suspected worms. However, when a third mentioned robbers, everyone immediately agreed that the beans had been removed by a human intruder to plant, eat, or sell.

The robber theory was invoked all year to explain missing items. If the loss involved something of real value such as a toy brought from home and reluctantly shared, a child might be blamed, but missing coats, beans, rugs, and sweaters were attributed to robbers. These malefactors seemed much like witches, but without magical powers, and were used to account for an endless list of mislaid possessions. Often, plans were devised to keep out or capture robbers.

Andy:	My father has two cactus plants in the big windows in his office. You know why? When robbers come in at night they touch the cactus plants and have to go back where they came from. To get the prickles out. That's why my daddy has those plants.
Deana:	What if you got stuck in the desert when you weren't stealing anything?
Eddie:	What if he stoled the whole cactus plant?
Andy:	Then he might fall on it and get stuck by it.
Tanya:	How about if the robber came in another way except by the way the cactus are?
Andy:	He can't. The doors are locked.
Tanya:	Does he have a cactus in all the windows? The robber could come through another window.
Andy:	Only if he has a ladder. And how can he open the window if the lock is on the inside? And if he tries to break the window he could cut his arm.
Wally:	They'll take him to jail if he breaks the window.
Eddie:	He could break through the door.
Tanya:	Then he might fall on the cactus.
Andy:	I'm going to tell my daddy to get more cactus plants for every window. And also one by the door.
Wally:	Hey, here's a great idea. Let's put a cactus plant by the lima beans the next time.

The robber feared by adults bears no relationship to the one created by the children. Their robber is so busy stealing lima beans he has no time to cause harm.

Man in the Moon

"We found the number-2 racing car!" Eddie was triumphant. This was the car I had searched for and had been advised to wish for instead.

"I wonder if my wish did it?" I asked.

"See, the piece from the Star Trek game went behind the cabinet. So we moved it. And we found it."

"It had nothing to do with my wish?"

"You couldn't see it," Eddie explained, "because it wasn't sticking out when you looked."

"Thanks, boys. By the way, how about the number-1 racing car? That's still missing. Should I wish for it?"

"You'd better just move all the furniture," said Warren.

Inconsistency is the norm, even in wishing. Before, I had been urged to use a magical solution, but now it seemed more sensible for me to move the furniture.

On the other hand, when Earl mentioned that you could make a wish on the man in the moon, the children earnestly examined the issues.

Earl:	My cousin says you can wish on the man in the moon. I told my mother and she says it's only pretend.
Wally:	He doesn't have a face or a body.
Lisa:	Then he can't see. He's not real.
Deana:	But how could he get in?
Wally:	With a drill.
Eddie:	The moon won't break. It's white like a ghost. The drill would pass in but no hole will come out.
Earl:	There can't be a moon man because there's no door. How would he get in?
Wally:	Maybe there's a secret passageway.
Teacher:	Who made it?
Wally:	The moon man.
Kenny:	There *is* a face but my daddy says when you get up there it's just holes. Why would that be?
Deana:	Somebody could be up there making a face and then when somebody goes up there he's gone.
Lisa:	He might have left a hole from last time.
Fred:	There can't be a moon man. It's too round. He'd fall off.
Wally:	He can change his shape. He gets rounder.
Eddie:	The astronauts didn't change their shape. They had oxygen for the air. In machines.
Fred:	I saw that on television. They were walking on the moon. But a real moon man would have to find a door.

	And if you fall in a hole you'll never get out.
Andy:	Sure you can, when the moon is a tiny piece.
Warren:	There *is* such a thing as a half moon. But the astronauts can't be cut in half. They can only go when it's round. A moon man can squeeze in half.
Wally:	That's what I said. He's a round shape or half a round. But I never saw a door.
Eddie:	There's no air there. No air! But air is invisible so how can there be no air?
Wally:	Only the moon man sees it. He makes himself invisible so he can see it.
Earl:	My cousin says you can wish on him.
Wally:	The moon is right next to God so he could talk to God.
Tanya:	Maybe there's a moon fairy, because some fairies are white that you could see through.
Lisa:	He could be a different kind of fairy—the kind for up there.

The credo at age five is to believe that which makes you feel good. Lisa once said there was no tooth fairy, but she continued to refer to all sorts of fairies. She may have been saying, "I know adults don't believe in fairies but I like it when the world has fairies."

As long as children are unsure of the boundaries between fantasy and reality, they will invent supernatural beings to protect them. When part of the moon disappears, children like to think of a moon man capable of adjusting to those strange circumstances and they like to talk about their ideas. Whether they do discuss them or not depends as much on the adult reception as on their own verbal ability.

After the discussion about the man in the moon, Wally said, "That gives me a good idea for a story."

> Once upon a time there was a little boy and he went out of the house and then his father got home. The father didn't see him and then he went out to find the boy. He thought maybe the boy flew up the moon because the boy was magic. So he went up there but still he didn't find him. He came down and went into the forest and saw a lion. He killed the lion with a gun. Then he found the boy. They went home.

"Was the father magic too, Wally?" I asked.

"No."

"The reason I asked is that he was able to go up to the moon to look for the boy."

"No, he didn't really go up. He only looked up there because he could see the boy's shadow if he was there," Wally explained.

"How about if the boy was hiding in one of the holes?" asked Warren.

"He wasn't," said Wally. After all, it was his story.

Theater

Even before we stepped on our new twelve-foot painted circle, Wally had invented a story about it.

> Once there was a magic circle in the forest and a giant lived inside. There was a boy and his sister walking into the forest. The giant tried to trick them because if you stepped inside the circle you turned into a spell. But he couldn't trick them so they went home and had supper.

In these few words Wally introduced our theater-in-the-round. The new stage was both necessary and symbolic; acting had become the major integrating factor of the day, encircling and extending every other interest.

We dramatized three kinds of stories: picture-story books, the children's own material, and fairy tales. Each served a different purpose, none was a substitute for the other.

Picture-story books offered flexibility, novelty, and brevity. They were instantly digestible and often quickly memorized.

The children's stories, lacking great plots and memorable prose, answered one of the children's most important questions: what do other children think about? Their stories resembled the informal dramatic play that went on all day and received the same intense concentration.

If the picture-story books permitted quick, pleasant accomplishment, and the children's stories encouraged spontaneity and human interest, the fairy tales set the tone and established the themes that enabled us to pursue new ideas and look more deeply into old ones. They also had the decided advantages of superior plot and carefully structured dialogue.

"The Tinder Box" was the favorite fairy tale. Except for the role of the witch, which I took whenever no one wanted it, the story seemed to have universal appeal. It tells of a soldier who returns from the wars and performs a favor for a witch, thereby gaining great wealth and instant obedience from three magical dogs. This soldier thinks nothing of cutting off the witch's head or of having the dogs attack the king and queen. Of course, in the end he marries the princess and becomes the king.

Teacher:	Why did the soldier have to cut off the witch's head?
Lisa:	Because she wouldn't tell him about the tinder box.
Teacher:	Did he have to kill her?
Lisa:	Otherwise she could change him into a frog.
Wally:	Or a rock.
Fred:	Anyway it doesn't even matter. She could come alive again. Witches can't be dead. They know magic.
Teacher:	Then why didn't she come alive and get back her tinder box?
Eddie:	That's one of the hardest things to do. It takes about a hundred weeks to do that.
Deana:	Why didn't the witch go down herself to get the tinder box?
Jill:	Then who would pull her up?
Warren:	Why didn't she get a ladder?
Jill:	Maybe she didn't even have a ladder.

Eddie:	A magic person can make a ladder appear.
Warren:	Witches have brooms.
Wally:	The soldier could hold her up.
Ellen:	Where could he get the ropes from?
Eddie:	From the witch. Wait a minute. She doesn't need him. She's magic.
Fred:	She could tell the soldier to get a ladder from the wars.
Tanya:	She might be tired from flying. She wanted help.
Lisa:	She might be in a costume.
Earl:	Why didn't she go to a witch's store, get a broom, and fly?
Wally:	She was afraid. Magic dogs don't like witches.

Though the children were intrigued by the possibilities of influence and power available to a witch, they did not often choose to portray her. On the other hand, nearly every boy and half of the girls wanted to be the soldier. I could not imagine performing the story fifteen times, however, especially if I was to be the witch.

"I don't know the fairest way to decide who will be the soldier," I said, "but we can hardly act it out fifteen times."

"Well, I asked first!" Wally called out, looking about him at the other raised arms.

"So what!" said Eddie. "We have to use the list."

"That's no fair then!" Kenny cried. "I'm always on the bottom."

"I'm at the top," Lisa reminded everyone.

"Girls can be the princess," said Wally.

"Girls can be anything they want!" Lisa, Kim, and Deana shouted out in unison.

"Hold on, please, all of you," I said. "I just realized: we *will* have time to do it fifteen times."

By the end of the year we managed seventeen "Tinder Box' performances, because Rose and Tanya decided they too would be the soldier. We had discovered an all-purpose hero, one who caused heads to roll in many a child's fable.

> Once a boy saw a lion in the forest. He said, "Give me all your gold or I'll cut off your head." So the lion gave him all the gold but he still cut off his head.

"Why did he cut off his head if the lion gave him all the gold?" I asked Wally.

"The lion was a bad witch in disguise." Wally had decided in several earlier stories that "a bad witch in disguise" was a convenient way to dispose of characters.

After Wally told his story, Lisa composed one of her own.

> Once upon a time there was an ugly witch. She wasn't ugly to her children. One day she said, "I think I will go outdoors and if the people say I'm ugly, I'll beat them up." But the people thought the witch was not so ugly. Then a soldier came and he did think she was ugly so he cut off her head. The children went for a walk in the forest and found another mother and she was nicer than the first one.

The key to the fairy tale, of course, is magic. Just thinking about magic was satisfying to the children. If, in addition, they could talk about it, act it out, and put it into stories, they had strong feelings of contentment, of being in their own milieu. Magic is always relevant; children pay careful attention to any words, either from another child or from a fairy tale, that may transmit magical information.

"We have to say the words in fairy tales the exact true way," Deana said one day. This was during an argument about the precise comment the soldier in "The Tinder Box" makes to the first magic dog.

"Right!" said Wally. "They're written by magicians. That's why!"

Not everyone wanted to dictate a story, but eventually everyone wanted to act in one. When Kim asked to be the soldier in "The Tinder Box," I was surprised, because she had refused all other speaking roles. She would accept a nonspeaking part in a classmate's play and might whisper a comment if a discussion was important to her. However, she was the only member of the class who had not yet spoken in a formal play.

She was shy. When a visitor asked her a question, Kim would lower her eyes and remain silent. The children would tell the guest, "She's shy." It was a simple statement of fact. Kim liked being the baby in the doll corner, the little sister in the sandbox, and the child who is read to in the library corner. Now she claimed her turn to be the soldier.

I introduced the story and for a change, one of the children accepted the role of the witch. "There was once a soldier who was on his way home from the wars. Suddenly an ugly witch jumped in his path."

Kim:	(*Silence.*)
Witch:	Say "What do you want?"
Kim:	What do you want?
Witch:	Can you do me a favor? You'll get rich if you do.

Kim:	(*Silence*.)
Witch:	Say "What's the favor?"
Kim:	What's the favor?
Witch:	Climb down this hollow tree and go to a place with a thousand lights and then you'll see a door. There's a big dog in there with eyes as big as saucers. He's on top of a box of copper pennies. Take the pennies.
Kim:	You forgot the apron.
Witch:	Here's my apron. Put the dog on the apron. Then take the money. But if you like gold better . . .
Kim:	Silver.
Witch:	If you like silver better go to the next room. That dog has eyes like towers.
Kim:	Millstones.
Witch:	Eyes like millstones. Take the silver. But if you like gold, go to the next door.
Kim:	Third door.
Witch:	Third door. There's the one with the round towers. You can have his gold. Don't forget to bring me the tinder box. My grandmother left it there.

(*Kim goes from dog to dog, placing each one on the apron and filling her pockets with coins.*)

Kim:	(*Silence*.)
Wally:	Tell her "Haul me up, you old witch!"
Kim:	(*Silence*.)
Witch:	I'll haul you up.
Kim:	Ask me, "Where's my tinder box?"
Witch:	Where's my tinder box?
Kim:	(*Silence*.)

Lisa: "To be sure, I've forgotten it."
Kim: To be sure, I've forgotten it.
(*Kim retrieves the box.*)
Witch: Give it to me.
Kim: Why?
Witch: None of your business.
Kim: TELL ME OR I'LL CUT OFF YOUR
                HEAD!
Witch: No.
Kim: THEN I'LL DO IT.
(*Kim swings her sword in the air and laughs as Act
One ends.*)

It is not easy to assimilate fairy tales. They must be heard
again and again. We read ours every day at rest time in a
darkened room with everyone stretched out on a mat. It was
a good way to do it. We didn't need to look at pictures or
look at each other; we listened to the words we would come
to know so well and imagined what the characters looked
like and what everything meant. I could tell that characters
appeared differently with each hearing, because our
discussions emphasized different qualities or feelings.

The first time we read "Rumpelstiltskin," for instance, Lisa
laughed aloud when the strange little man destroyed himself
in a fit of temper. But the following week she transferred her
sympathies. Rumpelstiltskin now seemed to be the victim. He
had, after all, saved the life of the future queen by enabling
her to spin gold out of straw. The promise of her first baby
did not seem too great a sacrifice.

Lisa: She's really not nice!
Teacher: But he wanted her baby.

Lisa: Why couldn't she just share the baby? Or wish for another one? Because he was really her friend.

Warren: She didn't even know him.

Lisa: If you *don't* know each other you act nice. You don't argue.

Warren: If you *do* know each other you act nicer.

Lisa: Wally and Eddie fight and they're best friends.

Wally: We don't really fight. But if someone is a stranger then you really do fight because you think you're better than him.

Lisa: You don't even bother with a stranger. Anyway Rumpelstiltskin was a friend and he helped her make real gold. He was *lonely*. Lonely! That's why he was stamping and screaming.

Teacher: Lisa, do you remember the first day of school when you didn't want your mother to leave? You stamped and screamed like Rumpelstiltskin.

Rose: You were lonely, right?

Lisa: I was little then. That's why.

Babies

I am always tempted to make direct connections between the children's stories and comments and the information I have concerning their family life. Wally's tendency to picture fathers in threatening roles suggested a parallel to his own experience because there was no father at home. Yet Warren, with an affectionate and attentive father, dictated similar stories. Teachers need to be wary of jumping to conclusions.

Even so, when Lisa wanted the queen in "Rumpelstiltskin" to share or give away her baby, I was certain that her mother's pregnancy was responsible. The report of an expected baby usually sent me looking for the latest sex education book. However, in the face of what I interpreted as Lisa's ambivalence, I decided to wait. It was fortunate that I did; the children's fantasies were more useful than my facts. They were useful to me because once again I was alerted to the kinds of facts children will not accept. And they allowed Lisa to discuss her ideas and experience the comfort of sharing the same views as her classmates.

> *Lisa:* I think I know where the mother gets the bones, the blood, and the water to put in the baby.
>
> *Deana:* What's the water for?
>
> *Lisa:* For crying.
>
> *Deana:* I think everything just grows inside of you.
>
> *Lisa:* *Before* it grows. She gets bones from dead dinosaurs and blood from a dead person and water from a glass of water.

Deana:	People can't collect bones. God does it. He gets the bones from cave men.
Eddie:	They're just your own bones. My dad has a bible book and it tells about the first man and woman that were ever on earth and God made every-thing, even the water and blood and bones. I think God does get them from dead people. No, wait. How can that be? No one is even dead before the first person. So it must be from dinosaurs.
Jill:	My mother says parents make their own children. How can people make people—all by themselves? God has to do it. I think my mother was asleep when it happened.
Tanya:	God makes new bones out of old bones, but not the broken ones. He gets blood from those.
Fred:	The blood evaporates up to the sky.
Akemi:	Bones and water and blood come from the sky. Jesa send it. Mother make it baby.
Warren:	Akemi, first you have to make a wish. Then Jesus makes it grow inside her stomach.
Andy:	The baby is inside of an egg shell. Then you get bigger and you crack open the shell and they take you out in the hospital and give you blood. It comes in bottles.
Wally:	God uses egg shells and bones. He makes everything very small. First the angels bring up the dead people from

the dirt. Then God takes the things he
needs for new people.

The sky gives and the sky receives. Even Akemi, who
seldom trusted her English sufficiently to speak in long
sentences, felt confident enough to explain the heavenly
source of life's essentials.

By the time the child has learned about God and heaven,
he accepts the idea that all sorts of used items disappear
upward. His earliest perceptions include steam and smoke
rising into the air. Couldn't this also be the way bones, teeth,
blood, tears, even Christmas trees find their way back to
God? The world is seen as a giant recycling plant with heaven
as the storage area and God as the distribution manager.

A few days later Tanya continued the discussion as if there
had been no interruption.

Tanya: I know where the milk comes from.
            I *saw* it. When my Aunt Frieda had
            her baby I saw the whole thing.
Lisa: I know about it too. My mother
            told me.
Tanya: She puts her chests into the baby's
            mouth and—
Lisa: They're called *breasts.*
Tanya: And he knows just what to do. He
            sucks it like a real nipple and there's
            sort of milk in there.
Lisa: It's *real* milk.
Tanya: This is where the milk comes from:
            the mother drinks a glass of milk and
            it goes into her breast and the baby
            thinks it's a bottle because he keeps

Lisa: his eyes closed and then he just drinks
it up.
And if the mother has coffee the milk
part goes into the baby, right?

New milk comes from the familiar milk in bottles, new bones from old bones, and new blood from used blood. Direct connections are developed and awkward gaps ignored. Jill's lament, "How can people make people?" is more complex. The very notion sounds unstable and upsetting. Such disturbing "facts" must be redesigned.

When Lisa brought a book about babies for me to read, the children listened closely and then gave their own interpretations:

Deana: What's that other place the baby stays
in?
Teacher: The uterus.
Deana: The father puts a seed in there.
Lisa: It's a tiny fish.
Teacher: It does look like a fish, the way the
artist drew the picture. It's called
sperm.
Eddie: I know something about sperm but I
don't think it's polite.
Teacher: Go ahead. Say it.
Eddie: Well, the father sticks his penis into
the mother's vagina and the sperm gets
going.
Lisa: The baby is squeezed inside a circle.
Warren: What do they use the seed for? Does
it grow into a fish?
Lisa: That's the fish. It's for food.

Tanya: When the mother eats something it
             falls right in the baby's face. It
             makes him cry.
Lisa: It can't. He's inside the egg shell.
Teacher: Don't forget, we said the baby is in
             that special place next to the stomach.
             He doesn't need to worry about food
             spilling on him.
Tanya: But the stomach takes up the whole
             space!
Teacher: There's still room for the baby in
             that place called the uterus,
             remember?
Eddie: Hey, here's a really good idea: if
             the mother eats a white watermelon
             seed she has a girl baby. But if she eats
             a black seed she has a boy baby.
Lisa: My mother doesn't eat watermelon.
Eddie: Does she eat cantaloupe? She can do
             it with cantaloupe.

Lisa's book did not refer to a "seed," but the term is
commonly used in early talks about babies. The sperm in her
book were pictured swimming toward an egg, and the
fish-image was unshakable, as was the belief that the fish
provided food for the baby. In later conversations, however,
no one mentioned seeds or fish and the children returned to a
more familiar context.

Tanya: My other aunt wished for a baby.
Teacher: Did her wish come true?
Tanya: We don't know. It's still in her.
Teacher: How did the baby begin to grow
             inside your aunt?

Tanya:	She's old enough to wish for a baby.
	She's past high school.
Teacher:	Can the father wish also?
Tanya:	He tells the mother to wish.

Because wishing influences the outcome of this important event, the children find it useful to speculate about a variety of possibilities. However, the father's biological role is impossible for the young child to understand. Even simple diagrams are confusing, and children who are taught explicit terms will invent "watermelon seed" stories as readily as those friends whose magical beliefs are encouraged. The "facts" are rejected even as they are repeated; ideas so disconnected from familiar images will not be accepted.

A fetus inside a female figure is to the child a picture of a very uncomfortable-looking baby in a circle. However, when the child is simply told that a baby grows inside its mother, with no picture to intrude, he is free to imagine the baby residing in a number of cozy, maternal settings. He develops scene and story line to suit his needs at that particular time instead of being cut off from his fantasies and instincts by abstract symbols. Of course, he also is free to imagine the food splashing down on the baby's face, but the wishing principle can come to his aid and help him make the event conform to his wishes.

Lisa:	Do plants wish for baby plants?
Deana:	I think only people can make wishes. But God could put a wish inside a plant.
Teacher:	What would the wish be?
Deana:	What if it's a pretty flower? Then God puts an idea inside to make

	this plant into a pretty red flower— if it's supposed to be red.
Teacher:	I always think of people having ideas.
Deana:	It's just the same. God puts a little idea in the plant to tell it what to be.
Lisa:	My mother wished for me and I came when it was my birthday.
Deana:	The plant knows how it should smell and when it is supposed to come up.
Lisa:	The lima beans have the idea of *not* to come up. I think because it's too cold outside.

Wishes and ideas are interchangeable. The child hopes that his wish has the power to influence an event, so he may respond to an adult's question with a wish instead of a factual observation.

I introduced a guessing game designed to test children's notions of the laws of probability. A dozen cards were laid face down on the table. The children knew that ten were marked with a red square and only two with a blue square. The cards were continuously mixed up, and the child was to guess the color of a card before turning it over. Wally predicted blue every time, yet he always turned up a red square.

I asked, "Why do you keep choosing blue when there are so many reds and only two blues?"

"I know that," Wally answered. "I just *want* blue to come up. I'm wishing for it to come up."

The five- or six-year-old is at a singular period. He is not a captive of his illusions and fantasies but can choose them for support or stimulation without self-consciousness. He has become aware of the thinking required by the adult world but is not commited to its burden of rigid consistency.

Fish

Wally's stories might be used as a calendar in our class. Thanksgiving must be coming, one could say, because Wally is putting Squanto into a story.

> A boy walked into the forest and met a hunter. "I'm Squanto," said the hunter. "Have you seen a lion?" "Oh, I just saw a lion behind the tree," said the boy. So Squanto killed the lion and then the boy went home with Squanto and they ate supper. Then they lived happily ever after.

Wally told his first Thanksgiving story without enthusiasm, as if it were an obligation to be gotten out of the way. After I read several Indian legends, however, Wally returned to the subject eagerly. The mystical aspect of Indian folklore acted as a catalyst, stimulating new ideas.

> Once upon a time there was an Indian and the Indian was the most famous one in the whole wide

world. And his name was Kabuki and Kabuki got mad at the God of the Indians. The God of the Indians heard what he said and he was angry. And when he was angry he thought of a plan. And the plan was to trick him and get his peace pipe.

And then Kabuki met a Pilgrim. The Pilgrim was bad because he stoled some gold from the Indians. Then a tribe of Indians came along and they got mad at the Pilgrim because the gold he stoled was from the tribe of Indians. Then Kabuki signed a peace treaty with the Pilgrims and Indians. Then they had a Thanksgiving feast.

Indians must seem more heroic than Pilgrims, because most of the children chose to be Indians when we acted out the Thanksgiving story. They did, however, sympathize with the plight of the Pilgrims.

Andy:	The king said you can't go to your church. You have to come to mine.
Wally: ·	He wouldn't even let them be free.
Fred:	When the king tells you to come to his church, if the people don't want to they might build a boat and run away.
Earl:	You had to mind the king or he would hurt you.
Lisa:	They said they were fishermen, but they only wanted to fool the king. They brought all their things on the boat at night.
Wally:	They told their kids not to tell anyone or they would get put in jail. They were mad at the king for that. He wants them to be not very free.

Teacher: What does that mean, to be not very free?

Wally: They can boss you and make you do everything you don't want to do.

Lisa: Like my brother.

Eddie: The king didn't see them sail away but then they got sick and wanted to go back.

Rose: Why did they put the fish in the hole? Do they go fishing?

Teacher: Oh, you mean the Indians. Remember when I said they used small pieces of fish for plant food for the corn. They dug a hole for each corn seed and then they put a piece of fish in with the seed.

Andy: If they fished in the little holes they got more fish. They put a worm on the string.

Deana: See, they wanted the corn to taste fishy.

Wally: The corn seed sucks up the juice and when the corn grows it tastes like fish. It tastes sweet.

Tanya: If you bury fish it will grow into corn.

(*I start to review the function of the fish, but the specter of the missing lima beans stops me and I return to the story.*)

Teacher: What happened when the Pilgrims landed?

Kenny: They saw people with dark skins and they got scared.

Jill: They were afraid of the bows and arrows.

Wally:	The Indians were afraid of white people.
Andy:	Squanto told them, "Don't be scared. I think they're nice and friendly." And the Pilgrims thought they wouldn't be scared of the black people.
Wally:	Were they black people?
Teacher:	No, Indians. They also have dark skin.
Wally:	So the Indians made friends and showed them how to do all the things and build houses.

The historical narrative could be melted down to recognizable feelings and actions. Except for magic, all the elements of a good story were present: heroes, villains, escape from danger, loyalty, friendship. There was no need to invent bizarre behavior because every event could be pictured and acted out. The children could even place the concept of religious freedom within their experience of being ordered about by older people.

The problem with the fish story, by contrast, was that they could not imagine what happened to the fish. They might have been taught to say, "The Indians used fish as fertilizer," but they would still see a wiggly fish growing into a tall corn plant. The changing of fish into another form made no more sense than the disappearance of the lima beans.

Next year, I decided, I would skip over this odd detail that served only to distract and confuse. For the same reason I would try to avoid books dealing with sex education. If a child brought such a book to school, of course, it would be important to read parts of it, but only after the class had ample opportunity to discuss such topics as blood, bones, and watermelon seeds.

One aspect of the fish discussion that pleased me was my own reaction. Rose had asked why the fish was put in the hole. "Do they go fishing?" she wanted to know. Instead of thinking, "There goes one of Rose's questions again," I correctly anticipated that everyone else would have the same question. I was learning to trust Rose.

I had become aware of the large amount of time Rose spent in close attention to other people's conversations and stories. She listened to stories as they were being dictated almost as often as she played in the doll corner. She was beginning to copy my style of questioning the story teller; when Wally told his Squanto story, Rose asked him, "Was the boy an Indian?" and "Didn't the boy have his own father to live with?"

Rose went a step further; she began to question herself. She modeled her own Thanksgiving story after Wally's but asked herself a question following each line. Her answer then became part of the story.

> A girl said, "Can I go for a walk?" Who'd she say it to? Her mother. "Okay, you can go." She went to the forest and saw Squanto. Who's Squanto? An Indian. "Do you want to live with me?" Yes, she did. She asked could her mother come too? "Yes."

From the first day of school Rose showed how much she cared for people by questioning them about their feelings: Are you sad? Are you being punished? Are you lonely?

Now Rose asked questions about words and stories. When we read *Tico and the Golden Wings* again after Thanksgiving, Rose asked, "Why did the wishingbird give Tico golden wings?"

"Because he dreamed about them," answered Lisa.

"No," said Rose.

Lisa tried again. "Because he wanted them?"

"No."

"What's the reason?" Lisa asked.

"Because they were friends."

Later Rose dictated a new Tico story.

> There was Tico with black wings. Then he had a dream of a wishingbird. "I wish for golden wings." "Could you be my friend? Then you can have golden wings." "Okay. I'll be your friend." Now he has golden wings.

Some children would have Tico give up his dream; for others he is a giant-killer who needs no one's approval. Rose, however, rewards Tico because he is a friend. For the sake of friendship alone he may keep his golden wings.

Santa Claus

Christmas was building up momentum in the outside world, but Santa was still not part of the children's stories. Instead there were sad accounts of boys and girls deprived of presents, as in Lisa's story.

> Once upon a time there was an old lady who lived in England and she had two granddaughters who

were very bad. And it was a very mean grandfather who loved to spank children because he was mean. He took their cat and threw it on the ground. He said, "You granddaughters cannot have any Christmas presents."

Ellen's story was not much lighter in spirit.

Once there was a little girl and it was Christmas. Her mother said, "Go upstairs and do not fight and do not dirty anything and do not peek!" But then she broke the clock and Santa Claus only brought one tiny present.

Wally made his story short and forlorn.

There was a boy who lived alone so no one gave him Christmas presents and so he decided to live in the forest.

The stories reminded me of my grandmother's evil-eye precautions: pretend you have nothing to be happy about so the evil spirits do not become jealous.

Part of the reason for Santa's questionable role may have been his loosely defined position on the hierarchy of wish fulfillers. First came God, whose services were singled out for "hard" wishes. When God was busy he asked a fairy to help out—a tooth fairy or a "passing fairy" as in "Maybe a passing fairy will hear your wish." Only then might someone mention Santa Claus, but not with a great deal of certainty. I wondered: was Santa considered as trustworthy as a fairy or was he more like a magician? I suspected the latter, for the children did not speak of him as though he were subject to their control.

Another worry about Santa concerned rules. The child knows that in the absence of rules he himself may be the loser. There are specific circumstances under which rewards are gained. Most children have strong feelings about what should happen at Christmas, even as they covet everything in sight.

Eddie:	We saw Santa Claus yesterday at the store and he gave us presents and it wasn't Christmas day. He's not supposed to do that.
Earl:	Maybe he's just nice.
Eddie:	He's not supposed to do that.
Wally:	Maybe it wasn't Santa Claus.
Eddie:	He was real. He talked.
Wally:	The real Santa waits until Christmas.

Things that come too easily are viewed suspiciously, for they may indicate that wishing is unnecessary. If the wish loses its power, the child must relinquish his dream of control and be ruled by the whims and willfulness of others.

When the librarian told the children they could make a wish at the end of her story, there was total approval. She gave them a specific task: good behavior during her telling of a story. Their wishes would take a year and a day to be realized, thus creating a second task: patience. Best of all, the long delay in gratification relieved the child of the worry of immediate anticipation and possible disappointment, providing instead the distant prospect of well-being.

The librarian's plan paralleled the design of the fairy tale. The hero performs several specific acts—moving a mountain, killing a giant, stealing a bag of gold—and is rewarded with half the kingdom, to be claimed at an unspecified time in the future. There are no fears of being disappointed, for if the king changes his mind, another task, equally attainable, will be arranged for the brave youth.

Christmas is not that simple. Santa's demand is "good behavior" as defined by the adult. Wishes will be granted or not granted on a given day on the calendar. Moving a mountain is a "real" task and easy to imagine. However, "goodness" has too much to do with mood and circumstance: is the child a submissive Tico on a certain day or is he an arrogant Superman?

The unasked question seemed to be: can you trick Santa Claus? With this in mind the children set up a foolproof list of "bad" behaviors.

Ellen: Santa Claus knows if you're bad
             or good. If you're bad he doesn't
             give you any presents or maybe
             just one. If you're good he gives
             you lots.
Teacher: What would be so bad that Santa
             would not want to give even one
             present?
Wally: Taking all the Christmas presents
             and candy around the tree.
Kim: Pushing everyone in your family
             down in front of the tree.
Eddie: Kicking all the presents in your
             city or street.
Andy: Hitting or choking all the people
             in your building.
Earl: If a boy had his favorite toy and
             his brother stoled it.

Tanya:	If you run away from your mother.
Lisa:	If you hid and when everyone went to bed you took all the presents and all the ornaments.

Such wicked thoughts were safe because no one would actually perform these deeds. The items that might appear on Mother's list—arguing, fighting, refusing to go to bed or to clean your room—were not included. Earl came close when he suggested stealing a brother's toy, but made his brother the villain.

Descriptions of wickedness came easily, and there was an almost endless vision of calamitous behavior. The mood changed, however, when I asked the children to talk about good behavior. At first, good acts were limited to the absence of bad ones: not breaking windows, not stealing presents, not knocking down people. Then a more conventional view emerged: raking leaves, setting the table, minding mother. But when Kim gave yet a different response, there was instant recognition of the deeper quality of her approach.

Kim:	I'd be good if I went upstairs by myself because I'm afraid to do that and I don't do that.
Deana:	If I fell out of my bed and hurt myself because I was having a bad dream and I went right back to bed, that would mean I was being good.
Warren:	I would sleep tight and not get out of bed.
Jill:	I wouldn't come into my mommy's bed at night.

Kim had placed the sacrifice-reward motif of the fairy tale in full view. To relinquish a habit that one is afraid to give up, to perform a painful act of courage—these are tests one must pass to win half the kingdom or, in this case, mother's approval. When the subject of "badness" was resumed, the children dealt with more urgent material.

Eddie:	If you get all those toys on TV you want, Santa thinks you're bad.
Wally:	You *are* bad if you have all that junk in your room.
Jill:	Greedy. You're selfish.
Teacher:	Why selfish?
Jill:	Because you're not supposed to have all those toys and then you get yelled at to put them away.
Teacher:	How did you get all those toys in the first place?
Eddie:	From too much wishing.

Too much wishing is against the rules. Pestering, greediness, and impatience must not be rewarded. The child fears that punishment will follow such indulgence. He does not understand that it is the adult who is excessive, any more than he realizes that adult anger and punishment are not always his fault.

When Rose told us she saw a black Santa Claus, the discussion that followed was on a more confident level. Once again the children felt they were in control, as they debated the rules of fantasy and fairness.

Rose:	I saw a black Santa Claus and a white Santa Claus.

Kenny: He can't be black. He has to be only white.

Rose: I saw him at Sears.

Warren: Santa Claus is white.

Wally: If you're black, Santa Claus is black, and if you're white, Santa Claus is white. But I think he's white.

Teacher: But aren't you black, Wally?

Wally: I know. But I see Santa Claus and he's white.

Deana: There's both kinds. Because we went to Sears and saw a white Santa so the black one must have been sick.

Earl: He's very white. My sister said he's a spirit and spirits are white.

Teacher: Why can't a spirit be black?

Earl: I'm not black so I don't know.

Tanya: I haven't seen a black Santa Claus but I know he could be there, because everything comes in black or white. (*She looks around.*) Or Japanese. Or Chinese.

Eddie: No. I know only one color he should be. White. I saw him in the store.

Teacher: But Rose *saw* a black Santa.

Eddie: He could have been dressing up like a black Santa.

Wally: Did he talk, Rose? Maybe he had wires.

Rose: He said, "Ho, ho, ho!"

Wally: I think he was real.

Tanya: If he was real that means someone was dressed up like Santa Claus because he lives at the North Pole and he can't come here. Maybe he

	has other people meet the children while he stays there.
Teacher:	Is the Santa at the North Pole white or black?
Tanya:	There's two. The white Santa Claus goes to meet the children and the black one stays at the North Pole.
Wally:	He's magic.
Andy:	Wally's right! He changes colors. That's how it's done.
Eddie:	Now I get it! He's a magician.
Tanya:	See, someone must be dressed up to be a certain kind of Santa Claus. If they need a white one, *he* comes out. If they need a black one, *he* comes out.

Harmony is reached step by step, as logic mixes with sympathy:

1. Rose sees a black and a white Santa Claus.
2. There is a general consensus that Santa Claus is white, but the group must account for Rose's data.
3. Wally feels that black children ought to believe in a black Santa Claus, but he finds it hard to do so.
4. There is both visual and moral justification for a black Santa Claus, so there must be two Santas.

The invention of a dual magical Santa is a high order of rationalization made possible by the five-year-old's ability to use fantasy as a legitimate vehicle for thought.

Fantasy was equally helpful to Deana as she expressed some complicated feelings about God. We had just come from a school Christmas party when Deana told this story:

> Once upon a time there was a baby and another baby. One was named Susan and one was named Kathy. They were two little girls. They were special little girls. They were girls of God. When God died they would become God. Their mother was unhappy when God died. The angels led the two little girls until they had a new mom and dad. One of the little girls could fly to the heart and one couldn't. They still loved each other even though they were both pretty. They were both as pretty as ebony. Then the new baby came and that was the brother of God. It was named Sylvester. Sylvester became the new God after the sisters died with the angels.

How powerful and awesome is the young child's imagination. What fragmented images from the outside world have sifted through Deana's fantasies to produce such a story? Yet similar ideas are heard in the doll corner, and the children do not seem surprised.

Pulley

When we returned from winter vacation, there was a seventy-five-pound bag of sand on the floor in the middle of our circle. The bag was inside a basket, and I could not move it without scratching the floor.

"Look where Mr. Prentise left our new sand," I said. "How are we going to move it over there by the wall?"

"Too bad Superman isn't here," said Wally, laughing.

"Sure," added Andy. "He'd pick it up with one finger and in a second it'd be in the sandbox."

"Wait," Eddie called out. "How 'bout this? He'd give one look at it and it would melt right into the sandbox."

"No, he'd fly up to the roof and let it smash through all the floors into the sandbox." Lisa was laughing so hard she could barely get the words out.

This was obviously not a problem to be solved by Superman, nor did the solution lie with Santa Claus or the magicians. It was proper and natural to make Santa a magician to explain a black Santa. Christmas, after all, must not be the result of adult caprice. Self-protection also made it essential to invent a robber to account for the disappearance of the lima beans. A world that allowed things to vanish mysteriously could be a world in which you or your mother might become lost just as incomprehensibly. But magic was not appropriate in every situation. Moving a seventy-five-pound bag of sand required the kind of thinking used for measuring rugs and fixing broken toys.

> *Teacher:*   Well, since Superman isn't here,
>   what shall we do?
> *Eddie:*   I can do it easy.

(*He pulls on the handles of the basket and moves it about an inch. Everyone who wishes is given a chance to move the sand, and each child has great difficulty, all the while insisting it is easy.*)

Lisa: Do it with a rope. I can do it
          easy if you tie a rope to my arm.

(*She ties a rope to the basket and strains as she pulls on it, but the basket does not move.*)

Lisa: This is hard. The rope is too
          heavy.
Rose: Use a string.
Teacher: Here's some string, Rose. Try it.
Rose: I can't tie.

(*I tie on the string and the moment she pulls it the string snaps.*)

Wally: I knew that would happen.
Rose: How did you know, Wally?
Wally: Real workers never use string.
Kenny: Let the whole class pull.
Teacher: That's too crowded. Try four
          children. Kenny, Rose, Ellen,
          Fred—you try.

(*They pull and push in all directions and the basket moves slightly.*)

Rose: You made a scratch.
Ellen: Oh-oh! We're scratching up the
          floor.
Teacher: Then we must think of another way.
Eddie: Get a lifter to lift it up. Then
          wheel it up.

The children begin to visualize a pulley. They lack the vocabulary to describe the machine they are about to "invent." It is obvious that they have seen a pulley in operation, and they know it can solve their problem but they

falter and grope for the right words. As they speak, they act
out the movements of the pulley, swinging their arms up and
down and imitating a rope going around a wheel.

Andy:	Take a basket, a round fence, put the basket in there. Put it around a metal fence and lift it up or down. See, you have to pull it down.
Deana:	I think I know what Andy means. He means that there's a rope on. Put the rope on something metal and then pull the rope down so the rope goes down and the basket goes up.
Andy:	That wasn't what I mean. Get two ropes. Pull it up and the rope goes up. Pull it down and the rope goes down.
Wally:	Take a big crane and hook it up there on the ceiling and let the crane take it over to that side. A person sits inside the crane and controls it.
Teacher:	How could we get a crane into the room?
Wally:	Okay, just hook the crane to the ceiling—not the whole crane.
Lisa:	I didn't tie the rope to my arm. I forgot to do that.
Earl:	Not to your arm. Tie it to the table and pull the table.
Eddie:	No, look. Tie the rope on to a wheel and if we turn the wheel it would go that way, to the other part of the room.
Teacher:	Eddie still likes his idea of a rope going around a wheel.

Eddie:	I like Wally's idea too, but I like mine better. Get a rope, put a hook on the wall. Then tie the rope to it. Then pull it up on the thing that moves packages.
Warren:	I've got a wheel in the country. I can bring it. I'll ask my mother.
Earl:	Wait. Put two wheels together—wind them up and pull it sideways.
Kim:	Put it in the wagon.

After we try all the rope ideas, I suggest that we ask the high school science teacher for help. The children explain the problem to him and describe their solution of ropes and wheels.

"You've invented a very useful machine," he tells them. "We call it a pulley." He returns after lunch with a lightweight pulley and helps the children move the sand up on the wagon.

Although the mechanics of a scale may have been beyond the children's imagination, they could envision and describe the work of a pulley. They fumbled for words, but the problem was visible and the technicalities could be acted out.

A week later, with the pulley still in the room, I asked the children to solve a new problem involving a heavy weight. I stood on a long board and told them that they were to raise the board *while* I was on it, but without touching me.

"Why?" asked Eddie.

"Why do I not want you to touch me?"

"No," said Eddie. "Why do you want to be lifted?"

"Oh. Well, there's no real reason, Eddie. I just want to see if the class can figure out how to do it. It's a bit like a puzzle."

Eddie's question was logical; my request did not make the

kind of sense he had come to expect from me. The class was accustomed to dealing with genuine issues that needed to be resolved: Was Rumpelstiltskin a friend? What should be done when Tanya says "No ma'am" instead of "Yes ma'am"? Is there a black Santa Claus? How shall we measure the rugs? Do stones melt? How can we move the sand? Can you become a mother lion? Now they were to consider a strictly academic problem.

I did not anticipate a long discussion, because I was certain someone would ask for the pulley and solve the problem. Instead, they went through a step-by-step reenactment of the original drama of lifting the sand bag, but this time it led in a new direction and had a different solution.

Once again each child tries to lift the weight. Then they decide to do it by pulling on a rope. There is no mention of a pulley. Now a new approach becomes popular: the board is to be positioned above the floor. Lisa is the first to realize the possibility. She places a book under each end and, failing to lift the board, suggests that the books are not high enough.

Lisa:	Blocks are higher. Use blocks.
Deana:	Not those. Bigger ones. The board has to be *way* off the floor. C'mon, help me. Never mind, it's too heavy.
Wally:	Put the board on the table. Can we?
Teacher:	I don't mind. But look, the board is getting higher and higher and it's still just as hard to lift it with me on it.
Kim:	We need a . . . (*She makes "seesaw" movements with her arms.*)
Eddie:	A seesaw! We need a seesaw!
Teacher:	Can you make one?

Andy: Use a barrel. My brother made a
            seesaw on a barrel.
Teacher: We don't have a barrel. Could you
            use blocks?
(*The lever has been "invented." The children take
turns lifting me but don't comment when I move
the fulcrum closer to my side.*)
Teacher: Why do you think I moved the block?
Jill: You like it that way.

The pulley was not mentioned, perhaps because lifting a
teacher with a pulley seemed silly—or even frightening. Then
again children tend to focus on the first suggestion offered
during a discussion. This is a major reason why successive
examinations of a problem can take such diverse routes. The
children instinctively began solving both weight-lifting
problems by using their own bodies. Although a pulley was
used in the interim, no one saw its application in the new
situation. The use of a "machine" was a last resort.

It seemed appropriate at this point to visit the local science
museum for a demonstration of simple machines. There the
children were asked to solve a problem: to move a heavy
weight from the floor of the stage to a nearby wagon. A
museum lecturer directed the process and, with the help of
wheels, levers, ramps, and pulleys, the task was
accomplished in twenty minutes.

Later that day I told a story. "Once a caveman went into
the woods to pick berries. When he returned he found that a
huge rock had rolled down the hill and stopped in front of his
cave. He tried but could not push it away. He called his
friends to help but it was too heavy. The man said, 'I wish I
could think of an easier way to move the rock.' What advice
could you have given him?"

Fred:	Dig a hole under the rock and crawl in that way.
Lisa:	Get all the people and all the dinosaurs to push.
Wally:	Take a hammer and keep chopping until it gets a bigger hole.
Warren:	Go find another cave.

The adult should not underestimate the young child's tendency to revert to earlier thinking; new concepts have not been "learned" but are only in temporary custody. They are glimpsed and tried out but are not permanent possessions.

Numbers

The children could imagine the pulley and the lever in action, but there was no way to dramatize a spring scale. The free-swinging balance scale, however, is simple enough to be made by a child, and its concepts come across easily: up means lighter, down means heavier, as on a seesaw. The child can think about "light" and "heavy" without numbers to distract him.

We are surrounded by numbers—on calendars, scales, thermometers, clocks, and rulers—but these carry little information about measurements for young children. Numbers are a source of confusion if used for teaching science or math concepts. Light and heavy, cold and warm, minutes and hours, short distances or long—these measures are understood only within the context of action. Children do not grasp their meaning through numbers.

"We have three 12s in this room," Wally said one day. "A round 12, a long 12, and a short 12." Everyone at his table looked at him expectantly. "The round 12 is the boss of the clock, the long 12 is on the ruler, and the short 12 is on the calendar."

"Why is the 12 on the calendar a short 12?" I asked.

"Me and Eddie measured it. It's really a five. It comes out five on the ruler."

"You mean it's five inches from the edge of the calendar?"

"Right. It's a five." Wally stared thoughtfully at the clock. "I'm like the boss of March because my birthday is March 12. The 12 is on the top of the clock."

This numerical confusion became more apparent when we collected apples to make applesauce. Cards numbered from 1 to 22 were taped across the top of the piano. It was understood that each child was to bring one apple and that therefore twenty-two children would bring twenty-two apples. We would then make applesauce.

We amused ourselves for several days with math games based on the number of apples on the piano on any given day. We pretended the apples had fallen from a tree, rolled away, or were taken by a squirrel. If the number of apples to be counted in the game was less than five, there were no errors; up to ten, there were minor mistakes. After ten, however, number answers tended to be chosen randomly.

The source of confusion seemed to be the printed numbers themselves. Each apple was placed above a number on the piano. If there were five apples and the squirrel hid apples 2 and 3, the children saw at once that three apples were left.

When eight apples were on the piano and the squirrels stole 4 and 6, there was far less accuracy. But most children understood that the answer should be smaller than eight, and quite a few used their fingers for counting.

However, as the total passed ten, the numbers called out were chosen at random. If there were fourteen apples, and 3 and 10 were removed, the children used numbers above and below fourteen indiscriminately. They forgot their most dependable math skill, counting, because the printed numbers blocked this natural instinct.

When our collection of apples was complete, we removed the numbers and played some of the games again. This time the children did not hesitate to count the apples, sometimes touching them as they counted off the numbers out loud. Their confusion was gone.

We still had the pulley and took turns pulling up heavy items. Lisa and Rose decided to put the apples into the basket and lift them back up on the piano. At the time there were twenty-two apples.

"We have fifty apples," Rose declared.

"We counted twenty-two this morning, Rose," I reminded her.

"I know, but this is a bigger pile." For Rose "fifty" was another way of saying "bigger pile."

Lisa used "eighty-two" to mean "heavy." She asked if she could weigh herself on the spring scale, and I showed her that the scale stopped at twenty-five pounds.

"Do you weigh more than twenty-five pounds?" I asked.

"Much more," she said. "I weigh eighty-two." Lisa probably weighed no more than forty pounds, but it is typical of this age to pick any big-sounding number to represent one's weight. No significance is attached to the number chosen.

Tanya, for example, was considerably heavier than Lisa—perhaps by as much as twenty pounds. One day Eddie was pulling Lisa in the wagon when Tanya jumped in.

"Get out, Tanya!" Eddie shouted. "You're too heavy."

"I am not! How much do you weigh, Lisa?"

"Sixty-five and a half," Lisa told her.

"Well, I'm twenty-five. That's smaller."

"I don't care," Eddie replied. "You *look* heavier. I can tell." Eddie did not ask Tanya how *she* could weigh twenty-five pounds if Lisa weighed sixty-five pounds. He accepted the number she gave as he would her phone number or address.

My lack of faith in formal weights and measures as teaching tools did not always prevent me from using them, either out of habit or out of curiosity. One day we were reading Leo Lionni's *Inch by Inch* in which an inchworm goes about measuring animals. The book doesn't spoil a good story by imposing measurement tasks on the child, but as I read about the inchworm moving along a toucan's beak, Wally began to bob his head in short intervals.

"The beak is eight shakes long," he announced.

"Get the ruler, Wally," I said. "Let's see how long it is in inches."

He brought the ruler and measured the beak. "I was almost right. It's after the eight a little bit."

A few months earlier, Wally had "proved" the relative rug sizes by his "walk, walk, walk, walk," a technique similar to the one he used to measure the beak. He had understood that a normal walking stride could provide a useful measuring device. Now, by moving his eyes and head along inch by inch, he was copying the idea of the ruler.

Perhaps this *was* a good time to reintroduce the ruler. As I continued to read the story, we came to a page where the inchworm measures a pheasant's tail that is so long it overlaps the next page. Placing the ruler on the tail, I asked, "Which is longer?" Everyone saw that the tail was longer.

"Well, the ruler is twelve inches long. See the 12? Then how long is the tail?" I asked. When the first six children answered "twelve inches," I eased out of the quiz and returned to the story. They are daydreaming, I thought, or they heard a different question.

A page later, Earl suddenly said, "Fourteen inches." I turned back to the pheasant's tail and once again put the ruler on the page.

"How did you figure that out, Earl?"

"Well, you see," Earl explained, "after the 'twelve' I counted quietly in my head—'thirteen,' 'fourteen'—then I stopped."

"I say fourteen also," said Eddie. "Here's how I did it. I measured with my eyes as long as the tail kept going."

Deana was even more specific. "I saw the spaces on the ruler and I went one space, one more space, and one more space."

Now a few children began to call out answers—"sixteen inches," "nineteen inches," "twenty-five inches," any number bigger than twelve. These were the children who liked to recite large numbers. Even Eddie, who had already given us a correct answer, but wanted to demonstrate his knowledge of big numbers, said "fifty-two."

"I wonder why," I asked, "so many of you said twelve inches before?"

"For no reason," Wally replied. "I was thinking of twelve inches is all."

Wally had asked his own question—how long is the beak?—and had found the answer without a ruler. Had I really helped him and the others by bringing out the ruler? I had taken charge of the inquiry and hurriedly offered the conventional method. The research scientist would have waited longer and let the imagination have more play.

Still, I wondered if the ruler was becoming more "real" to some of the children, especially those who were actng out units or measurements in one way or another. I asked each lunch-table group to measure its table so we could tear off the right amount of poster paper from the big roller in the art room. The paper would become tablecloths for our Martin Luther King, Jr., birthday party in a few days.

"What should we use for measuring?" asked Deana.

"Each table can decide," I answered.

Table one measured "four rulers." Table two, three big blocks and one medium. Table three, three wood pieces. Table four, one long string. We placed the four measurements side by side on the rug.

Eddie:	Hey! They're all the same end!
Teacher:	What does that tell us about the tables?
All:	They're the same.
Teacher:	Which idea would be easiest to carry upstairs to the art room?
All:	The string.

The rulers, blocks, scrap wood, and string sidestepped the issue of numbered inches once again. The children were not ready to choose numbers to represent their ideas.

Apparently the rules of games seemed as capricious as numbers. One day Eddie and Andy invented a game with continually changing rules. The boys made a checkerboard design on a large cardboard, printing numbers, letters, and stars at uneven intervals. Each player then tapped an orange juice can on the floor a certain number of times, then moved a corresponding number of spaces. I watched through several turns but could not see how the game was played. Suddenly Andy announced he was the winner.

"How come?" asked Eddie.

"Because I got on the 20 in four turns. That's how you win."

Andy, in fact, had not had four turns, and during his third and final turn he had moved randomly around the board, but Eddie accepted the ruling. "Let's play again!" Andy insisted.

"I can't understand how the game is played," I said.

"You knock six or eight or eleven times," Eddie explained, "and then that's how many times you go."

"But how do you decide whether to knock six or eight or eleven times?"

"See, you tell yourself to do it six or eight or eleven times," Andy answered quickly. "Then you do it. Or if you think 'five,' go five spaces."

"But not 'seven'," said Eddie.

"Why not?"

"It's not in the game."

I looked at the board and 7 indeed had been left off. "There's no 13 either," I pointed out.

"Then you can't think 13," said Eddie.

Martin Luther King

Social rules, however, were not supposed to be changed arbitrarily.

"Can I be Martin Luther King even if I'm not next on the list?" asked Wally.

"You'll have to talk to the class," I replied. "Tell them why you want the rule changed this time."

We had gathered on the circle to act out the first of three events in the life of Martin Luther King. The story of King's struggle evoked strong feelings among the children. The indignities of being told where to sit, where to play and with whom, where to go to school, and where to eat seemed to echo some of the children's own complaints. No other historical narrative was retold by the children with such fidelity or acted out so often.

Wally:	Here's the thing I want to know.
	See, I want to be Martin Luther King.
	But it's not my turn. So is it okay?
Eddie:	Why do you want that, Wally?
Wally:	Because my mother saw him once. And my grandmother too.
Eddie:	That's a good reason. Okay, I agree.
Everyone:	Me too.

Wally had been the first to talk to me about King. "Next week is something very important. Do you know about it?"

"Do you mean Dr. King's birthday?"

"My mother told me to bring you this record. She says you'll like the speech about the little daughter."

In this speech King describes his young daughter's feelings

when told she cannot enter an amusement park called Fun Town because she is black. Near the end of the speech King says, "Yoki, even though you can't go to Fun Town, you are just as good as anybody who goes into Fun Town." Whenever one of the children repeated that line, the class cheered just as the audience did on the record. Wally wanted to be Yoki's father, reassuring his sad child.

Wally had been taught to feel a close kinship to his people that most five-year-olds did not have yet. He was conscious of his own racial and personal attributes and identified other children by theirs in an easy, natural way. His was a unique contribution to a kindergarten class.

"Give it to the black girl in the red dress," he would say, before he knew everyone's name. Or, "Tell the white boy over there it's his turn." He told Akemi he liked her "Japanese paintings" and Warren that he liked "Chinese eyes." He found out from Earl why "kosher Jews" could not have milk with meat sandwiches and from Tanya that her mother thinks she is fat and won't allow her to eat "junk."

Wally's message to us was: I see your differences clearly and I want you to see mine. It's okay to be different; in fact, it's nicer that way.

Five-year-olds often do not know that their special qualities and differences are acceptable in school. They must be told, and Wally's way of telling was to look closely at people and talk about their traits with as much interest as if they were characters in our stories.

When Wally told us he wanted to be Martin Luther King, everyone knew this was not an attempt to appear better than other black children who might wish to play that role. His was an act of personal identification.

In addition to the Fun Town episode, we dramatized the Montgomery bus boycott and a scene from King's childhood.

White
neighbor: What do you want, Martin?
Martin: I came to play with Tommy.
Neighbor: Well, he can't play with you
              anymore.
Tommy: Why not? Martin's my friend.
Neighbor: No. You can only have white
              friends now because you're
              going into first grade.
Martin: (*Goes back home.*) Tommy's
              mother chased me away. She
              slammed the door.
Mrs. King: I didn't want to tell you,
              Martin, but some people slam
              the door on different colors.
Martin: Why?
Mrs. King: Some white people don't like
              colored skins. They even have
              a law about that.
Martin: When I grow up I'll make them
              stop.
Mrs. King: That's hard to do.
(*The play is interrupted by a spontaneous discussion.*)
Wally: They did that because he
              was black like me. My mother
              said they learned the wrong
              way from *their* mothers.
Teacher: What would you have done, Wally,
              if you were Martin?
Wally: Go play with my other friends.
Teacher: You wouldn't have told your
              mother?
Wally: That's being a tattletale.
Rose: You *are* supposed to tell about
              bad things, Wally.

Warren: Just slam the door on that bad
           neighbor.
Eddie: Call the police.
Wally: Just say to Tommy's mother:
           they are people and you are
           people so you can both play.
           If he does anything bad, send
           him home and tell his mother.

The children made no racial distinctions in acting out the
stories—King, Rosa Parks, white neighbors, black bus
riders—all parts were taken according to the class list
without comment, although Wally explained why he was
glad he was to be white on the Montgomery bus. "I don't
want to be bossed," he said. Then he told us again the details
of the bus strike.

Wally: My mom said Martin Luther King was
           smart and he decided about having
           white people to sit in the front and
           black people in the back. Wait! That
           was what *they* decided. And then *he*
           decided to throw off that sign and so
           you could sit anywhere.
Eddie: You forgot to say about Rosa Parks.
           See, she came on the bus and gave the
           bus driver some money and she sat in
           the chair and the bus driver said, "No,
           you're not white." And she said, "I
           don't care. I want to sit because I'm
           tired and also I gave you a dime." Was
           it a dime or a nickel?
Tanya: Maybe a quarter.

Eddie: Maybe a dime. So she said, "I'm not going to leave." So they put her in jail.

Wally: Now you can sit wherever you want. Also Martin wasn't allowed to go to any water fountain or any bathroom and he also had to have only a black grocery-store man to pay. He was separated. My mom knows all about that. She even used to *be* separated.

Eddie: We're talking about the bus now, Wally. He told people they shouldn't go on the bus and don't pay them money. Then if they get a broken bus they can't fix it.

Warren: And he told them to stop shopping if you can only be white.

Wally: I want to tell the part about when he was in kindergarten. Tommy's mother said, "Go away, bad boy." And he said, "I'm his friend." And she said, "No, you're the wrong color." He was only a little boy so he cried. So he went to his mother and she said, "I have to tell you something sad. There's a rule against us."

Rose: Why did they have that?

Wally: It was their habit. Anyway Martin changed all the rules.

Lisa: All the *bad* rules.

Fred: But not the one for the bathroom. The girls have to separate from the boys.

The concept of skin color as a cause for discrimination was

confusing, but the general idea of unfair treatment was understood by everyone.

Deana: Tommy's mother was mean to Martin. Very mean.

Eddie: She wanted to boss him. My daddy does that to me *always*. He blames me and he closes the door on me.

Teacher: What does he blame you for?

Eddie: For no reason.

Deana: Did even Martin Luther King have to sit in the back of the bus?

Teacher: All black people did.

Deana: That was really no fair.

Jill: That reminds me. Why do we have to always sit at the same lunch table?

Teacher: What would you rather do?

Jill: Sit anywhere we want. That's more fair.

Teacher: That might become confusing. Most people would rather know exactly where they sit, Jill.

Deana: I don't would rather know.

Eddie: Me neither.

Teacher: How does everyone else feel about this?

(*There is unanimous approval.*)
             Well, then, it's okay with me.

Jill: Free at last!

Birthdays

Whenever children discover that a tall child is younger than a short child, they believe that somehow a mistake has been made. Bigger has to be older. I had known this for a long time, but I had not realized that you are bigger on the very day that you are older—on your birthday. On Rose's birthday she told us she was much taller, and every child in the class agreed.

Teacher: Do you mean taller since yesterday?
Rose: Because I'm six.
Wally: Yesterday she was five. She *is*
             taller today.
Lisa: On that very day when it's your
             birthday you're bigger. If I was
             four and on one day I got to be five,
             I'd be much bigger.
Teacher: Then would you have to wait until
             your sixth birthday to grow some
             more?
Eddie: Otherwise how would you grow
             bigger?
Teacher: Rose, could I measure you? I'll put
             this mark on the board. Now, where do
             you think the line was yesterday, when
             you were still five?
(*She puts a mark several inches lower. The
others put theirs even lower.*)
Teacher: Okay. Let's do this a different way.
             Kim, could we measure you? Pretend
             tomorrow is Kim's birthday. Today she
             is five and tomorrow she'll be six.

Put a line at the place Kim will be
when she wakes up on her birthday
tomorrow.
(*All the estimates are well above the original mark;
some are six or seven inches higher.*)

Teacher: Then must you get new clothes?

Eddie': Sure. Everything was too small on
my birthday.

Lisa: When you start running it makes you
have more energy. It makes you
stronger and bigger every day. But on
your birthday is when you grow
inches.

Teacher: Fred, you're the only other child
here who is six, so we'll ask you.
We didn't see you on your birthday
because it was during vacation. Did
you *feel* taller on that day?

Fred: I really *was* taller. My bed was too
short. I'm getting a new bed.

No matter how long the children discussed the question,
the conclusion remained the same. It is as if there is a
conspiracy to protect a communal belief from any contrary
evidence. The teacher may wonder: shall I bring out the
ruler? I can prove beyond any doubt that a person does not
grow instantly taller in one day. I will measure our next
birthday celebrant the day before and on the day of his
birthday, proving my point conclusively. The trouble is that
children do not confer legitimacy on the ruler. We can insist
that the children repeat our "fact"—this brings them our
approval—but we cannot force-feed a concept before there is
trust in the premise.

Body growth may also be thought of in terms of power and

influence rather than as lines on a stick. A better approach
might have been, "What can you do now that you are six?"
But even this question might have elicited fantasies of
superstrength, the wish being taken as the fact.

Language too has an invisible dimension for children.
Akemi's preoccupation with learning English led us into
conversations about language in general. I saw again how
certain abstractions can block the child's path between cause
and effect.

> *Teacher*: Why are there so many different
> languages?
>
> *Lisa*: Because some people don't know these
> other languages.
>
> *Kim*: They can't talk the way we talk.
>
> *Eddie*: Maybe when people are born they
> choose the language they want to know
> and then they go to a special place to
> learn it. I mean their mother chooses.
>
> *Andy*: Like a child could tell his mother and
> father to take him to a place where
> they can learn French if they are
> French.
>
> *Warren*: God gives people all the sounds. Then
> you can tell you're in a different
> place because it sounds different.
>
> *Wally*: When you're little you try to think
> of what the name of something is and
> people tell you.
>
> *Eddie*: Oh, yeah. Your mother tells you. You
> come out of her stomach and she talks
> English to you and she tells you the
> name for everything.

Deana:	If you live in a different country, there's a different language there. Wherever you were born you talk in that language.
Warren:	Wherever your mother was born.
Teacher:	Your mother was born in China, Warren, but you speak English.
Deana:	Because he never lived in China.
Warren:	I'm going to go to Chinese school on Saturdays when I'm six.
Eddie:	Someone has to teach you. My brother didn't know one word when he was born. Not even my name.
Earl:	When I was little I said "ca-see."
Rose:	What does that mean?
Earl:	"Take me in the car." Now I know every word.
Rose:	Me too.
Teacher:	Akemi was born in Japan and she speaks Japanese. How are you learning all these English words now, Akemi?
Akemi:	I listen to everybody.

As the children got closer to their own experiences they became more logical. "Why are there so many different languages?" is the sort of abstract question that prompts answers such as Lisa's: "Because some people don't know these other languages." Then Wally changed the emphasis of the discussion by describing how a little child learns an object's name. The implied new question—how do you learn a language?—was understood at once. Now the children did not need to guess at meanings, because the subject involved a concrete part of their own development. They had all learned a language; they could explain themselves in clear sentences.

When Akemi began to print Japanese words and tape them to the walls, two new questions came up. To answer the first, the children employed reverse-order logic, in which the effect is taken as the cause. But the second question was straightforward, and dramatic enough to enter Wally's stories.

First question: Why are there so many different alphabets?

Tanya:	Because all the alphabets don't start with the same when it's spelled.
Akemi:	Other country's people don't read English.
Kim:	Some people are English.
Rose:	Because when Wally made my letter, he made two lines here and another line there.
Eddie:	If there was only one alphabet God might not have invented towns like China or Japan or America.
Lisa:	There are different people. They got born in different places so they are different.
Warren:	They can't read it if it's in a different alphabet. They'd have to have a big discussion what that could be.
Jill:	Some people don't know the other people's language.
Andy:	They have a different voice.
Deana:	Then how could people understand?
Wally:	Otherwise you wouldn't even know what country you were in.

Second question: If you were in charge of the world,

would you make only one language or many languages, the way it is now?

Tanya: One language. Oh yes! Then I could understand everyone in the whole world.

Eddie: No, let it stay this way so different countries keeps on being not the same. Then you take trips to see what those countries are like and how they talk.

Ellen: I like the world the way it is but I don't like fighting.

Teacher: Is that because they have different languages?

Ellen: Well, if they can't understand each other they might think good words sound like bad words.

Wally: She means like if someone says, "Let's play," in French, then in Chinese they might think he said, "Let's fight."

Warren: Keep it this way because if you're Chinese you would have to learn English.

Teacher: Would English have to be the language everyone learns?

Warren: I don't know what God likes to talk. Wait, I changed my mind. Let everyone say the same language. Then when my mommy and daddy speak quietly I could understand them.

Tanya: I changed my mind too. Better not have the same language. Here's why: whenever this whole world had

	the same language everyone would say they want *their* language to be the one everyone has to have. Then everyone would blame someone else for giving them the wrong language.
Akemi:	If everyone speak Japan, everyone have to live there. My country too small for the big America.
Warren:	Everyone can come to China. It's much bigger. Let Chinese be the language. No, I changed my mind. Let my mommy and daddy talk English *all* the time.

An "I know what she means" or an "I changed my mind" says a child has recognized a truth and is stretching after the special meaning it may have for him. When children question each other, arguing or agreeing, it means they are listening carefully. They want to know about experiences they have in common with another child; they are curious about what has happened to someone else because it may also happen to them. When there is no such interaction, it is a signal to me that the children do not understand the subject.

Wally had a story about languages.

A little boy lived all alone in a deep forest. When he wanted to know a word he asked lions and tigers and wolves. They told him pretend words because he couldn't speak animal language. One day he saw a lady and a man who didn't have a little boy.

"What language do you talk?"

"Animal pretend talk."

"That's okay because we can teach you people's language. Which one do you want to learn?"

"English."

"Good, because that's our language. What words do you want to know?"

"Lion, tiger, and wolf."

"You already know them. You just said them."

"Then animal pretend talk must be English."

So they lived happily ever after. But the man and lady knew some words the boy didn't know, so they did have a lot to teach him.

Akemi

Rose, Kim, and Akemi began school with language problems, different in nature but similar in consequence; they could not explain their ideas easily. Rose lacked practice in putting consecutive thoughts into completed sentences; she had not understood the exacting connections between ideas and words. Kim's vocabulary and sentence structure were well developed, but self-consciousness in public often made her withdraw and bury her thoughts. Akemi's language problems stemmed from a vastly different cause. Having mastered one language, she alone of the three knew the pleasure of easy communication and was loath to flounder and stumble in a new language.

For all three girls, the lure of becoming a character in a

story proved stronger than their resistance to public speaking. This attraction seems almost magical. If the child's belief in magic is based on the assurance of being changed into something else in the future, then dramatics is the immediate representation of this idea.

Play provides a similar opportunity but lacks the powerful certainty of outcome. The printed story, whether by an adult or a child, promises dependability. The soldier will always kill the witch; the lost child will invariably find his parents; everyone will live happily ever after.

Stories have yet another magical quality: fully developed sentences borrowed from someone else. The dialogue can change a child from inarticulate embarrassment to confidence, as if by a magic wand. The only task required is to memorize the words. With enough practice, anyone can do this, because the practice is part of the reward.

"Akemi does not permit herself mistakes," her father had said on the first day of school, "so she won't practice English." He watched his daughter as she sat alone, drawing with her new school crayons. "If she learned English better she wouldn't be so disagreeable with the children. She was so angry when the nursery school children did not understand her."

The Nakamotos had come to America from Japan the year before. They were disappointed with Akemi's adjustment to school. "In Japan she loved school," Mr. Nakamoto continued. "She reads and writes in Japanese like a seven-year-old."

Mr. Nakamoto was right about Akemi. She was not comfortable with the children and she was afraid to speak English. What neither of us foresaw was the speed with which she began to use English in order to act in a play.

The first character she wanted to be was the woman in *The*

Funny Little Woman. This Japanese folktale concerns an old woman's attempt to retrieve a rice dumpling that rolls through a crack in the earth down to a place where "statues of the gods" live alongside monstrous creatures called "wicked oni." The old woman tricks the oni, steals their magic rice paddle, and returns safely to the world above.

The old woman's habit of saying "tee-hee-hee" made Akemi laugh despite a determined effort to remain the solemn outsider. She took the role immediately and produced a barely audible "tee-hee-hee," but it was enough to make her wish for more.

"Read me," she would insist, following me around with the book in her hands. Each time I read the story, Akemi repeated more of the dialogue. "My dumpling, my dumpling! Has anyone seen my dumpling?" became Akemi's leitmotif. She had accomplished her first complete English sentence, and since everyone knew the story she did not have to explain herself further.

By Monday of the second week, Akemi was ready to add to her repertoire. She walked directly to the library corner without depositing her lunchbox in her cubby and began leafing through a pile of books. When she came to *A Blue Seed*, our only other Japanese story, she examined it carefully.

"If I be this?" she asked, pointing to the fox.

"Can I be the fox?" I repeated her question.

"If I can be fox?" she asked again.

"Yes, you can. We'll read the book at piano time."

Akemi's choices were uncanny. The funny little woman went about laughing "tee-hee-hee," the very thing Akemi would not allow herself to do. Next she was the fox screaming out, "Listen everyone! This is *my* house. No one can come in without my permission. Everyone get out at once!" What an opportunity for the child who fears that this schoolroom will never feel like *her* house.

I took four Japanese stories out of the library, but Akemi, after a quick glance, passed them by. Her commitment was not to Japanese stories but to magic. She wanted characters who looked the way she wanted to look and said what she needed to say.

In *Tico and the Golden Wings*, the wishingbird said the right words for Akemi. "I am the wishingbird. Make a wish and it will come true." From the wishingbird she went to Kurochka, the heroine of *The Little Hen and the Giant*. On her way to kill the giant, Kurochka said to everyone who got in her way, "If you don't stop laughing right this minute, I will gobble you up!"

"Drakestail" gave Akemi a couplet she liked even better. "Quack, quack, quack, when shall I get my money back?" Akemi carried her memorized lines around like gifts, bestowing them on children in generous doses. "Quack, quack, quack, when shall I get my money back?" she would say, dipping a brush into a jar of paint. Soon everyone at the painting table would be chanting along with her.

"I am the wishingbird," she said, flying gracefully into the doll corner. "I wish for a golden crown," Jill responded, whereupon Akemi delicately touched her head with an invisible wand.

Adults who go about quoting poetry seldom receive encouragement, but the children rewarded Akemi by repeating her phrases and motions. She correctly interpreted this as friendship. Whenever a child copied her, Akemi would say, "Okay. You friend of me."

Her triumph came just before Halloween. She wanted a witch story but none of the Halloween stories pleased her. She told the librarian, "Witch story but not Halloween," and was given *Strega Nona*, an Italian folktale about a kindly old witch who owns a magic pasta pot.

Akemi memorized the magic verse at home.

> Bubble bubble, pasta pot,
> Boil me up some pasta, nice and hot.
> I'm hungry and it's time to sup,
> Boil enough pasta to fill me up.

Wally came running over, "What's that from, Akemi?"
"Witch book not Halloween," she replied. "You can read."
"I can't read yet," said Wally. "Mrs. Paley'll read it to us."
By the end of the day almost everyone knew the entire verse, and Akemi was ready to tell her first story. "Now I telling story, okay?" In only six weeks, Akemi had become a story teller in English. "Is Halloween story," she began.

> One day four colors walking. But one witch sees four colors. Witch with four hands. Witch holds four colors. "Let go, let go!" Four colors running. Witch running. Four colors running home. Is Mother. Oh, good.

In Akemi's next story just two weeks later, she had made considerable progress.

> One day is magic cherry tree. A nice skeleton is coming. The cherry tree says, "We are playing," A black cloud is coming. The cherry tree says, "We are playing also." They are playing all day. The mother comes. "You are coming home."

On Rose's birthday in January, Akemi dictated a story to be acted out at Rose's party. "Rose is the magic princess," she told us.

> Once there is castle has everything. Even nine princesses and nine dogs. When winter comes the boy came and hurt the princess in the night except princess is magic and doesn't get hurt. And then two robbers coming take two princesses home and tied them up. The next night is good-guy prince but he is lost and the magic princess find him and marries him inside her castle because it is so beautiful. But then the bad king came and stole the magic princess but she is not afraid. The king is magic but she makes him unmagic so he can't use his magic. She makes him into a frog and makes herself into a magic shark and she ate up his castle. Then the good-guy prince comes back and she makes him magic too so he is never afraid forever.

Akemi was conquering English, and I was learning an important principle: magic can erase the experiential differences between children. It can make the difficult simple and the simple rewarding. Akemi's princess made the good-guy prince magic "so he is never afraid forever." When magic is accepted and encouraged, the children are not afraid to think and speak.

Fairy Tales and Superheroes

Akemi's nine princesses and nine dogs evolved out of "The Twelve Dancing Princesses" and "The Tinder Box." The often-read fairy tales spawned new stories in which the children put their established heroes into different plots. Deana combined the twelve sisters with a theme from "Jack and the Beanstalk" and added her own ending.

> Once there were twelve dancing princesses. They had no parents. Every day they had to milk their cow to get fresh milk. But one day it gave no milk. They had to sell Cherry. Oldest said, "We must sell Cherry. Youngest, go to the market and sell Cherry." "I don't want to sell her," said Youngest. So Oldest asked her friend to go. But the storekeeper said, "We cannot buy cows."

Deana enlarged on the original story, which tells nothing about what the twelve princesses did during the day. We know only that they danced all night. She also gave the youngest sister a chance to rebel, for in the fairy tale the oldest continually bossed the youngest.

Akemi combined "Rapunzel" and "The Tinder Box" in a story she called "The Tree Castle and the Princess and the Evil Witch."

> There was a tree castle and a princess was on top and no one could climb up because the evil queen lived underneath. The princess had hair long down to the ground. Magic box was by the tree. If you are striking once, cat coming. Twice, another cat. Threes, another cat. A good boy is finding the box.

He is striking three times, makes three wishes. First
wish: kill the evil queen. Second wish: bring down
the hair. Third wish: help the boy climbing up.
Then they finding the first mother and father who
were nice.

Wally put the "Tinder Box" soldier into Hansel and
Gretel's forest.

A soldier and his magic dog met a lonely boy in the
forest. "Are you hungry?" said the soldier. "I didn't
eat for a year," said the boy. "Here's a cake house.
Eat the windows." Then an ogre came. "One more
bite and I'll eat you!" The magic dog killed the ogre
and they all lived in the cake house and didn't eat
any more of it.

Fairy tales stimulate the child's imagination in a way that
enlarges the vocabulary, extends narrative skills, and en-
courages new ideas. Superhero stories, by comparison, are
limited.

Once there was Battlestar Galactica and it had
Apollo, Starbuck, and both of them had a Colo-
nial. They went to shoot the Silons. Apollo shot
twenty, Starbuck shot ten, Apollo shot the whole
base. Apollo shot the whole Silon plant.

Once Captain America has to kill Green Goblin.
So he smashes him. He gets a disguise. Captain
America kills him twelve times. He gets a disguise
again. He kills him again. Then more bad guys get
killed.

These stories give great pleasure in the telling and the acting, but they provide little opportunity to explore new ideas. Throughout the year the stories hardly changed. They were written in a fixed code, understood by everyone who watched certain television programs, and were reinforced daily in spontaneous play. Even those boys who were not allowed to watch those programs mimicked the action and played in identical ways.

Television images have a powerful effect, one that is too strong for adequate expression in words alone when the dramas are reenacted. As in play, the children use fragmented sentences and sound effects: "Take that!" "Got you!" "Ah-h-h!" "This is serious!" Often, the story teller cannot remove himself from the action.

> Superman is after the bad guys. Sh-sh-bam! Got them! K-K-K-K! Got you! Trying to get away? Let's get those guys! Watch out! Kryptonite! Hey! I need help. Here comes twenty bad guys. Hey! Crack their heads! Here comes fifty bad guys. Help! Never mind. They're dead.

Superhero drama is dynamic and satisfying, but the "good-guy-kills-bad-guy" format of September continued through June. The only change came about through bringing in a new superhero or killing more bad guys. The stories do not reflect the qualities of a particular child or encourage variations. If the child's name is omitted from a superhero story, the authorship is almost unrecognizable. This must be the point then, I decided. Such stories are used to mask, not reveal, individuality.

Yet I would not do without these noisy, "wild" manifestations of commercial television. They accurately represent the play style of young boys, where action counts more than words. The redundant adventures give legitimacy to rough-house play and meaning to the chase. Sometimes words are almost eliminated as the boys pursue each other with grunts, groans, and yells.

Nor would I eliminate the superhero from the classroom. For boys who need extra encouragement, the superhero tale is the perfect transition from the Bat Cave to the writing table. Boys who are too impatient to dictate a story will come willingly to write a superhero story. If in addition the boy knows that his story will be acted out, he will follow the teacher around until she is free to write down his words.

Wally, however, did not need that transition. He loved to playact Superman and Han Solo, and he told enough of these stories to keep his membership in the brotherhood active. But, for the most part, he mixed the events in his life with magical ideas and created a succession of stories uniquely his own.

Eddie preferred only superhero stories, but they did not sound as if they came from him. He was a thoughtful, articulate child with probably the largest vocabulary in the class. He was accustomed to hearing adult explanations and copied the same style in his own approach to a subject. Children such as Eddie are excessively admired for what they say, but often their words do not represent what they think. Frequently he would begin a conversation by espousing an adult point of view but switch over to magical ideas as soon as others introduced them. For Eddie, superhero immersion must have been a welcome relief from the high expectations of the adults in his life.

Eddie's large vocabulary may have caused him as much frustration as did Rose's limited stock of words. Rose and Eddie thought alike on most subjects, yet Eddie was expected to think like an older child. He had learned that the talk and play of his peers mirrored his thinking, but he also understood that his family considered this thinking "babyish." A cover-up was required: Superman to the rescue! The ritualized responses of the superhero culture protected Eddie from the "achievement" concerns of his parents. The rules and language of superheroes are private; adult logic and criticism are irrelevant.

For all their popularity, superheroes were restricted to play and stories. These powerful creatures seldom entered into our serious discussions. When real events and problems were considered, no one mentioned Superman. Even the boys, whose absorption in this play dominated the sound waves, knew the difference between play and real influence. A powerful and exciting superhero could not move a bag of sand or make a wish come true.

Monsters

Akemi was the only girl in the class who consistently chose to join the boys in superhero play. She was also the only girl to dictate a superhero story.

> Once there was a dog named Lassie and he's the strongest dog in the world. If somebody gets in trouble Lassie will help. One day Lassie is walking

down the street and everybody is saying "Help!"
It's a monster with a crashing noise, but Lassie
wins. Next morning is twenty monsters with twenty
crashing noises, but Lassie wins. Next morning
is a hundred and fifty monsters. Next morning
Lassie and all his friends turn into the biggest dinosaur in the world and fight a hundred-and-fifty-
mile big monster but Lassie wins.

Akemi's story was unusual for a girl. More typically the
girls made monsters harmless or denied their existence.
Deana's giant, for example, did nothing worse than steal
jumping beans.

There was a giant named Chris and he would always take a lady's jumping beans because he liked
jumping beans. The lady hated the giant but the
sister said, "Oh, there isn't such thing as a giant."
She said that because she never went out at night
and giants *only* go out at night. So one night she
did go out and she found a giant named Chris.

The purpose of Lisa's story seemed to be to discredit monsters.

Once there was a little girl. She lived with her sister
in a cabin with her mother. And they went outside.
The little girl was playing. She didn't see the sister
but she saw a monster. She caught the sister. "I saw
a big hairy monster!" "There's no such thing as
monsters." Then they went home.

The wolf in Jill's story may have come directly out of "The
Three Pigs," but she insisted it be ignored.

The big sister says, "There's no such thing as a wolf." Once the wolf was in the garden knocking down apples. One fell on the little sister's head. The sister ran inside. "There *is* such a thing as a wolf!" said the little sister. The big sister said, "Don't be such a silly." Then they had their supper and went to bed.

And Deana disposed of *her* monster by exposing it as a doll in disguise.

Once there were two sisters and they found a scarecrow. "I'm afraid," the two sisters said. So one sister said, "I can beat that scarecrow into fifty and a hundred pieces." Then they went home and told the mother. She said, "There's no such thing as a scarecrow." "We'll show you. See?" "Oh, that's not a scarecrow. That's only a raggedy doll trying to dress in a scarecrow costume."

Ellen created a dangerous situation but then devised a pleasant surprise for her principal character.

There was a little girl who lived with her mother and they didn't have enough food. "Child, if you go out and get some food, I'll love you," said the mother. "If you get lost you will be killed and I won't like that." So the little girl went out and was lost but was not killed. Then she saw a monster and she was killed by the monster. The monster gulped her and it was her father inside the monster's mouth. He'd been gulped too.

Characters in the boys' stories did not say, "There's no

such thing as a monster." Confrontation with a monster was the whole point of the story. Warren's monsters were visible to all and quite dangerous.

> A dinosaur smashed all the trees down. Gargantuan came out of the water and saw a boy walking in a forest. He killed the boy but the boy wasn't really dead because there was really a trap he fell into.

Not only did girls reject fierce monsters, they often dictated stories whose sole purpose seemed to be the avoidance of danger or conflict of any kind. Tanya's was a typical doll-corner story.

> Once upon a time there was a little girl. She asked her mother if she could go to the playground. "Yes," said her mother. She went to the playground and played on the swings and the slide. Then she came home, ate macaroni, and went to bed.

Tanya told her story after playing in the doll corner with Jill and Lisa, where the same purposefully calm, uneventful scene had unfolded.

> Lisa: Here's your macaroni, sister.
> Jill: Can I go to the playground, Mother?
> Lisa: Okay. (*She mixes pretend-food in a bowl.*) Hm-m-m. Here we go 'round the mulberry bush. How was school today? Did you call your grandmother?
> Jill: I'll make pizza. (*She pushes a rolling pin back and forth on a piece of rubber.*)

Lisa: You be the baby.

Jill: Cover me. (*She lies down in the crib
              and sucks her thumb.*)

Tanya: (*Enters on hands and knees.*) Meow.
              Meow. Meow.

Lisa: Let's take the kitty-cat for a walk.

Such an idyll might be interrupted by "bad" behavior: mean mother, naughty children, noisy animals—but no monsters from the outside. Serenity would be recaptured with the dependable rituals of family life: a flurry of food preparation, shopping, child care, and eating. Yet there *is* a monster lurking in the doll corner.

Lisa: Bad baby! You need a spanking! I'm
              locking you in your room.

Jill: (*She kicks and screams.*) Bad mommy!
              I hate you! I'm getting a new mommy!

Lisa: Who cares! I'm getting a new baby.

Jill: (*She begins throwing dress-up clothes
              on the floor.*) You're stupid!

Lisa: Bad sister! (*She spanks Jill, who begins
              running through the classroom.*)

Teacher: Girls! Stop that! You're too noisy!

Lisa: But she's being bad. I *have* to spank
              her.

Jill: I'm running away from home.

Underlying the tranquillity of the doll corner is a recurrent theme of disobedience and punishment. Doll-corner play, which seems so different from superhero drama, is really a variation on the same theme. Both the girl in the doll corner and the boy in the Bat Cave are vulnerable. The placidity at the kitchen table and the show of power atop the tallest building both create an illusion of safety that denies the child's fears. Another doll-corner story of Tanya's suggests this crack in the hearth:

> Once there was a little girl. The mother told the sister to tell the little girl not to go to the farm. But the little girl did. And she got lost at the farm. The mother said, "Where is your sister? I want to give her some vitamins." "She got lost at the farm." "There! I told her not to go. Your sister is a bad girl and you're not."

Monsters do not enter the doll corner, because the powerful figure who alternates between loving and hateful behavior is already there. The sisters and babies who stir up trouble are there, too. Superheroes, on the other hand, keep Mother, Daddy, and baby sister out of their domain; their battle is with the giant.

Little Sister vies with Mother to gain control of the doll corner, but it is the princess who is the female superhero. Princess and fairy are often interchangeable, as in Deana's story.

> Once upon a time there lived a beautiful fairy prettier than anyone in the world. She was married to a king. But one day she decided she didn't like the king and made him into a prince with her magic wand. Then they got married. The princess got a golden ring for her wedding. Then she got a rainbow sweater that was beautiful, made of golden silk. Her name was Princess Leia but she wasn't in Star Wars. One day a murderer came and killed her. She was never to be seen again. Then on an-

other day the fairy came to life by someone touching her with a magic wand. But the murderer was dead. The policeman caught him and put him in jail. Then the fairy made her fairy sister into a prince so she would have someone for her husband. They lived happily ever after and their whole house was made of silk.

Lies

The appearance of power, as denoted by the Superman cape, is as good as the power itself. A monster seen and then denied is as good as no monster at all. The affirmation of an event carries its own validity—so says the child, but the adult does not agree.

Few virtues in a child are given more importance than honesty. To most adults, it is unacceptable to suggest that the appearance of honesty is as good as the honest act itself, yet this is exactly the child's point of view.

"If you have not had a turn, raise your hand," says the teacher. A hand shoots up; it is someone who has already had a turn. To the adult this is a blatant lie. But the child may feel he has not had a proper turn or that others have had more turns. He may simply wish he had not had a turn so he can have another. None of this matters anyway, for if the teacher believes him he feels he has told the truth.

Eddie: I told my dad the truth. I was fighting
               with my brother and my dad came in
               and said, "Who did this?" because we
               made such a mess. We threw every-
               thing on each other and dumped the
               whole box on the floor. I said it hap-
               pened by accident.
Teacher: Was it an accident?
Eddie: Yes.
Teacher: But you said you did it on purpose.
Eddie: Yeah, but I didn't want to get yelled at.
Teacher: Did your father believe you?
Eddie: He really did. See, I told you it was the
               truth.
Teacher: Has anyone here ever told a lie?
Everyone: No! No!
Teacher: Let's act out a scene in which someone
               tells the truth just as George Washing-
               ton did when he cut down the cherry
               tree. I'll put these pictures on the table
               and, Wally, you take one picture and
               hide it. Then I'll ask who did it and you
               tell me.

*(I close my eyes and Wally takes a picture of Lin-
coln and hides it in his cubby.)*

Teacher: Oh, my favorite Lincoln picture is miss-
               ing. Who took it?
Wally: I did.
Teacher: Good for you, Wally. You told the
               truth.
Wally: I found it on the sand table. I didn't
               know who it belonged to.
Teacher: Wally, is that supposed to be the truth?
Wally: I didn't want you to say I stoled it.

Even in a role-playing game, Wally had to protect himself. Any response that shielded him from adult disapproval or punishment was a good and an honest response.

The same day, the subject of honesty came up again, but this time it was not simulated. The sand table was saturated with water, and the water was dripping on the floor. I had warned the children not to do this and I was angry.

Teacher: Who poured in all the water?
Everyone: Not me. I didn't.
Eddie: Maybe someone came in and did it
              while we were out.
Tanya: Maybe the sink leaked into it. That
              could happen.
Teacher: I would like to know who did it,
              please, so I can ask that person
              not to do it again!
Tanya: Maybe it was Eddie.
Eddie: It was not! Maybe it was Tanya!
Teacher: Okay, look. I don't care who did
              it. How can we make sure it
              doesn't happen again?
Wally: *You* put the water in from now on.

Anger from an adult and perhaps the fear of punishment make a child weak. Wally always liked to wet his own sand, but my irritation made him unsure of his ability to do it properly. I was certain that Eddie was the culprit because I had seen him overwater the sand table before. Yet Wally reacted as if he were guilty and expected to be punished.

Eddie had been a major cause of the drowning of the lima beans. I had said to him, "Eddie, you're not doing the lima beans any good with all your watering. Remember, we said only the Monday and Thursday leaders will do the watering?"

"I didn't water the plants."

"I saw you do it, Eddie."

"I was just bending over to look."

"Okay. If you see someone else watering them when it's not his turn, remind him."

I had been annoyed with Eddie for lying to me though I knew he responded in self-defense. I wondered if I could concoct a blame-free situation in which the abstract idea of honesty might be explored. Perhaps my first attempt, having Wally "steal" Lincoln's picture, was a poor choice; Wally knew it really was a favorite picture of mine.

I made up a new role-playing skit and explained it to the children.

Teacher:	Pretend a mother is going shopping and tells her child, "Please do not touch these tiny glass animals on the table. They are very delicate." The child promises, but as soon as the mother leaves, he picks one up and it accidentally falls and breaks. He can tell his mother the truth or he can say that the wind blew it over. We'll let the one who acts the part decide after we all give our opinions.
Wally:	Can I be first?
Teacher:	Fine. Wally will be the boy and Ellen can be the mother.
Ellen:	Don't touch my animals because they break easily.

Wally:	Okay, mom. I promise. (*He pretends to pick up an animal and drop it.*)
Teacher:	Come back now, Ellen. Tell him how you feel when you see your broken glass animal.
Ellen:	I feel sad. Why did you do it?
Teacher:	Don't answer yet, Wally. See what everyone thinks you should do first.
Eddie:	Tell the truth. She won't believe him about the wind.
Andy:	Tell the truth. Because he might be president.
Rose:	If he didn't tell the truth he should go to bed and stay there.
Kim:	If he shakes, his mother will know he's lying.
Akemi:	He should tell the truth because his mother gets mad. Mother says tell the truth. Lies are scary. Mother and father are thinking the wind can't do it.
Earl:	Tell the truth because his mother might get suspicious.
Eddie:	I changed my mind. He should tell a lie because what if his mother spanks him really hard like Jack.
Tanya:	I agree with Eddie. He shouldn't tell the truth. She'll never find out because he said he promised.
Wally:	I made up my mind already. I don't need any more ideas.
Teacher:	All right. Ellen, you come back again.
Ellen:	Why did you do it?

Wally:	I didn't do it, Mother. The wind must have blown it over.
Ellen:	Oh.
Teacher:	Do you believe him?
Ellen:	Yes.
Teacher:	But he's acting out the story I told, and in my story the boy *does* drop the animal and break it.
Ellen:	But this time it was different.

The appearance of an accident caused by the wind, if believed, becomes the truth. Let's pretend, they say, that this is what actually happened. If we pretend, maybe it will become what happened.

Teacher:	Once, a long time ago, I told a lie to a principal. My class was very noisy coming back from the playground and later he asked me if that was my class that made such a racket. I told him no.
Rose:	Why?
Teacher:	I must have been afraid he would think I was a bad teacher.
Andy:	I told a lie too. I said there was a pet in my closet but there wasn't.
Tanya:	When my daddy didn't want me to write on the walls, one day I did and told him I didn't.
Deana:	One day my mother told me not to eat candy and I ate it.
Eddie:	Once my brother and I were messing up the basement and I told my father it was an accident.
Teacher:	Was that a lie?

Eddie: Yes, because it really wasn't an
            accident.

It was not hard for the children to admit that they some-times told lies. Eddie understood that the incident he had de-scribed as the truth could be labeled a lie by someone else. But tomorrow it might again seem to be the truth.

Labels relate more to desire than fact. The "fact" is that Eddie would have preferred the mess in the basement to have been an accident, and Wally would rather the wind had knocked over the glass animal.

Most interesting, however, were the children's reactions during the skits. To them, once the drama began, the event was really happening. No matter what ground rules I had laid out, the misdeed had to be disguised.

Sugar

When Earl brought a sugar beet to school and announced that it was the source of sugar, it was difficult for the class to believe him.

Earl: Guess what! Sugar comes from this.
Rose: How does it?
Earl: My mother told me. You take a sugar
           beet, you cook some of it away, and
           then you press it out.

Deana: But this is a better way: get some
flour and mix it up with something
else to make it turn into something
else but it has to still look white
and feel like something else so it
tastes better.

Deana suddenly does not make sense. Her usual fluidity is
gone; it is as if she is not listening to herself. In this discussion
she is using words as Rose once used them—as if it doesn't
matter what she says. The others follow her lead.

Lisa: It has a little bit of flour and
then you start mixing it around with
a little bit of white stuff and you
cook it and it gets a little bit
harder and then you put something
hard in it and it gets to be sugar.

Wally: See, they put it in a big machine
and they let it do for a while by
itself. Then they take some stuff
and mix water in it but not too
much. Then they put it in the oven.

Eddie: You have to put honey into it first.
Then you mix the white stuff for
about a hour.

Earl: No. See, you have to have a sugar
beet. My mother said so. You take
the juice from it. Then you mix it
with the honey and flour. How about
baking soda?

Teacher: Earl's mother is right. We do get
sugar from sugar beets. Also from
plants called sugar cane. Let's
look it up in the library and see
how it's done.

We send Earl to the library, and he returns shortly with a book about sugar. I read aloud several passages, and we learn that sugar beets and sugar cane provide most of the sugar we use. The beet is first *soaked* in hot water and this draws out the sugar.

I cut the beet into small pieces, pour boiling water over it, and let it soak all morning. We all have a taste after lunch and discover that we have made a sweet liquid.

Teacher:	Too bad we can't do the rest. This is a picture of the machine they use to boil away the water part so only the sugar part is left. It comes out looking like white crystals, the kind we have in our sugar jar.
Eddie:	*Then* they mix it with flour and baking soda.
Rose:	How do they know if it's salt or sugar?
Eddie:	They take just a tiny bit of flour and mix it with some machine and then they cut up the sugar beet and cook it and they take a little bit of white stuff and the stuff you make Chinese noodles out of and they mix it with white sugar and put it in another machine and then it comes out like salt.
Deana:	Just taste it. You can easily tell. Salt is salty.
Ellen:	That's what the honey is for. To make it sweet.
Rose:	Put candy in.
Ellen:	Not candy. Honey.

| *Deana:* | Just taste it is all. I can remember how things taste even if I'm not eating them. All I do is *think* of something I ate and I can remember exactly how it tastes. |

(*Deana's language and thought return to their usual level the moment she considers a factor from her own experience.*)

Teacher:	Can you think about sugar and figure out exactly how it's made?
Wally:	Sure. You *know* it has to come from white things. So you think about white things. That's how you decide what it's made of.
Andy:	Not white shoe polish!
Fred:	Not white paint!

(*Everybody laughs and begins to call out white nonedibles.*)

| *Earl:* | Only food that's good for you. And first use the sugar beet. |
| *Eddie:* | We *know* that already. |

No one said, "I don't know." If flour, soda, egg white, and honey are not involved in making sugar, why would they think of these ideas? The experience of extracting the sugar in hot water provided a small clue, but the connection between sweet water and white sugar was still obscure.

The next day an additional causal relationship was suggested. We were measuring ingredients for Valentine's Day cupcakes. Lisa poured out a teaspoon of salt and said, "I really do know where salt comes from."

"Where?" asked Rose.

"From eggs. People shake salt into eggs. Then when they need salt they get it back from the eggs."

With this kind of reasoning, perhaps sugar, so often seen being put into recipes that use flour, baking soda, and eggs, might be retrieved from those items. This logic seemed familiar. It was, I realized, the same thinking that imagined a baby's bones coming from dinosaurs and new blood coming from old broken bones. That which goes up must come down and go up and come down again. And that which goes in *must* come out.

A few minutes later I poured a quart pitcher of flour into two half-quart pitchers so that the children could have turns adding flour to the cake mixture. I asked, "Which holds more flour—the first pitcher or these two?" Everyone at the table chose the two smaller pitchers, including Eddie, who had shown me one day at the sink that the pint bottle of water was exactly the same as two eight-ounce measuring cups. First appearances continue to make sense, it seems, when circumstances are altered. Later at the sand table, Eddie saw the relation between the quart and half-quart pitchers instantly.

Valentines

The children based their opinions about how sugar is made entirely on color and taste. Sugar, white and sweet, ought to come from other things that are white and sweet. It would be inappropriate to say, "A sugar fairy touches all the old cakes and cookies and takes the sugar out to make new sugar." The five-year-old understands that sugar is man-made, so he delegates a machine to do the work. However, lacking direct experience and the sugar fairy, the child flounders and grasps for any explanation. It doesn't matter if the explanation makes sense, because the process itself doesn't make sense.

A question asked on Valentine's Day allowed the children a better opportunity to see relationships, and therefore their speech was less ambiguous.

Teacher: What is Valentine's Day all about?

Tanya: Because it's about love and stuff and it shows how we love people.

Eddie: It's about your heart. The heart doesn't really look like a valentine but some people think it does.

Teacher: Why the heart? The body has other parts.

Lisa: The heart watches your blood in case you're bleeding too much.

Deana: A valentine looks like a heart and a heart looks like a valentine.

Eddie: If we didn't have the heart there wouldn't be anyone around. We're so happy we have a heart—that's why. If it stops beating, you die.

Deana: It just sounds like it should be your heart. It sounds good that way.

Earl: If God didn't make a heart your body might get a heart attack and you'll die.

Tanya: If you don't do something you're supposed to, God can make a heart attack inside your body.

Earl: If you don't have a heart, you don't have a heart attack.

Eddie:	You have to have a heart. It makes you alive.
Wally:	Who decided there should be a heart on Valentine's Day?
Eddie:	Maybe the government.
Lisa:	It has to be God because He made your heart.
Eddie:	God is not a person.
Lisa:	He *made* all the people.
Tanya:	There *is* such a person as God.
Rose:	He made the houses.
Eddie:	*Workers* made the houses.
Wally:	God made the workers, didn't He? So Rose is the same as right.
Teacher:	Tanya said Valentine's Day had something to do with love.
Tanya:	If you didn't have a heart you wouldn't have as much love as you would like to.
Wally:	The heart is the most important part of the body and it's the most for your love.
Jill:	If you don't have a heart you won't have the love that goes into your heart.
Eddie:	If there was not such a thing as a heart there wouldn't be such a thing as love.
Tanya:	God puts the happiness into your heart. He does it mostly on Valentine's Day and Christmas. He made Valentine's Day and Christmas to do that.
Wally:	The valentine is when your heart is happy even if you don't get toys. On

> that day you could be happy if you
> get lots of valentines but on Christ-
> mas you won't be happy if you didn't
> get toys.

There were no machines and abstractions to distract the children from thinking freely about God and their own feelings. They could make some sense out of what they had heard.

1. The valentine represents your heart.
2. God made your heart.
3. Your heart keeps you alive.
4. Your heart is a repository for love.
5. You are happy to have a heart that keeps you alive and full of love.
6. The heart is for happiness and love.
7. Valentines represent happiness and love.

During our Valentine's Day party, Tanya asked, "What if a person didn't get *any* valentines?" Eddie had a quick answer. "That would mean nobody liked them."

Teacher: How do you know if somebody likes you?

Tanya: When you think there's someone that doesn't like you . . . well, you don't have to worry about that so much. You could have some other friends.

Kim: Maybe they might not like you but later they will.

Fred: When they grow up they could be friends.

Ellen: If someone says to you, "I don't like

	you," and then you say, "I don't care," and then you know they don't like you.
Lisa:	When people think that no one's being nice to anybody you should just ignore them.
Teacher:	It sounds as if it's easier to talk about people who don't like you. But how can you tell if someone *does* like you?
Wally:	Watch a person and see if they stay and play.
Jill:	And lots of people get in fights and they act like they're not being nice but the next day they want to be friends again.
Eddie:	If he talks to you a lot he likes you.
Deana:	I can tell if someone doesn't like me. I like someone who doesn't like me. I chase him and he doesn't run after me. He tries to hit me and I duck.
Eddie:	I know the boy next door is my enemy because we know we're enemies.
Ellen:	They say bad words to you if someone doesn't like you.

(*In such discussions the children consistently
account for bad feelings first and then bring out the
good.*)

Deana:	Jill, remember when you and me were in your father's car sucking our thumbs?
Jill:	Oh, yeah. That was so much fun. My daddy kept singing, "Rockabye baby in the tree top." Remember?
Fred:	Hey, Wally. Remember at Eddie's birthday party we put those metal kettles on our heads?

Tanya: Lisa, remember when I first came to your house and I didn't know where the bathroom was? And then we put the boats in the bathtub?

Teacher: Are you children saying that you know someone likes you if you remember nice things you did together?

Ellen: Remember when we were looking for the black kitty at your house, Kim? And we said, "Here, kitty, here's kitty" and we were laughing so much?

Kim: And it was in the closet? I remember that.

Warren: Kenny, remember in nursery school we brought snow inside in our hats and the teacher was laughing?

Kenny: Hey, let's do that again. Okay?

The three questions brought about different kinds of thinking: How is sugar made? What is Valentine's Day about? How do you know if someone likes you? The first required the children to consider an unknown process in which an object completely changes its form. They combined magical thinking with random guessing, resulting in an unproductive discussion. In thinking about Valentine's Day, the children could make use of experience and reason. Though the heart is invisible it represents that which is known: life and love. Even images of heart attacks and blood did not distract the children from drawing logical conclusions. Their ease in using God as a catalyst helped them develop their thoughts.

However, it was the question on how to know if someone likes you that received the most thoughtful and mature responses. Of the three discussions, only the one about friendship could be reduced to solid experience. The fact that the children initially examined the opposite side of the question attests as much to understanding as to emotional bias. They were then able, with some help from me, to go beneath the superficial level of "if they stay and play" to establish a universal attribute: you know people like you if they remember sharing a good time with you.

A week later we acted out "Snow White and the Seven Dwarfs." Deana, as the wicked queen, said to Warren, the king's huntsman, "Take Snow White out into the forest and kill her. Bring back her heart, so that I will know you have obeyed me."

Rose looked startled. We had read the fairy tale three or four times, but this was the first time we were acting it out.

"Is it her heart?" she asked.

"He doesn't really do it," Deana said. "He pretends."

"Oh." Rose relaxed. "He could bring her a valentine." She looked around and smiled.

Tricks

One day I set up an artificial test of the children's magical beliefs. Our central bulletin board, the one we used for our largest paintings and story posters, had been decorated with children's valentines and stories. The week before, the children had helped me put white paper over a partly finished

Snow White poster on the board. I had said, "After Valentine's Day we'll take off the valentines and the white paper and finish the Snow White poster." The morning after Valentine's Day, I arrived early to remove the valentine display.

Later, I had begun to read a story when Ellen asked, "Where's the valentine board?" I was seized with an impulse to know if the children would believe an absurd story.

> *Teacher*: What if I told you that the valentine board was gone when I came in this morning even though it was still there when I went home yesterday. Would you believe me?
>
> *Eddie*: It's underneath!
>
> *Wally*: Must be.
>
> (*Wally and Eddie run over and lift a corner of the Snow White poster to see if the valentines are there. They seem unaware of the enormous difficulty in removing over a hundred thumb-tacked items and replacing them under the original poster.*)
>
> *Wally*: (*Surprised*) It's not here!
>
> *Teacher*: What if I said, "A valentine fairy came at night and took everything away." Would you believe me?
>
> *Everyone*: No! No!
>
> *Deana*: There's no such thing as a valentime fairy.
>
> *Eddie*: How could a fairy even get in at night?
>
> *Jill*: Through the walls.
>
> *Lisa*: Through a small crack in the door. Fairies can make themselves very small.
>
> *Jill*: The fairy could break a window and then fix it right away.
>
> *Warren*: It would be too heavy.

Eddie: Not if she made it invisible.
Deana: She can make it all fly out of the
              window.
Teacher: Wait, wait! I was only joking. I
              came in early and took everything
              down. Look, it's in this box.

The children seemed disappointed; once the image of the fairy appeared, it was obviously such a pleasant prospect that they would rather believe it than not. They were saying, "We wish it *had* happened this way." I do not like to trick the children, and I did not do it again.

When Wally said, "I've got three big brothers and four sisters," it seemed necessary to challenge him. I did not want the children to falsify certain kinds of information, such as family facts, with me.

"Wally, your mother told me that you are the only child in the family."

"Oh, yeah. I forgot."

"Maybe you'd like to have a lot of brothers and sisters."

Wally did like the idea of a big family. He was not tricking me; he was wishing aloud. Perhaps "I forgot" meant that he forgot this was the sort of data you relay accurately to adults. Soon after this, Wally dictated a story about a large family:

> There was a little boy with no mother and no father. But he had seven brothers and seven sisters. The brothers were called dwarfs. The brothers lived in the forest and Snow White came to visit but she didn't stay. She said, "One Snow White mustn't live with seven brothers." So she looked for the seven sisters. A magic bird came and took her there. It was sixty miles away. They were glad

to see her. They ate supper and went to bed in seven beds.

Later Eddie "forgot" that leaves are not taped to trees. We had seen a movie about a boy who was so sad to see the leaves fall from his favorite tree that he made paper leaves and taped them to the tree.

At lunch I asked Eddie, "How *do* leaves grow on trees?"

"Trees grow from roots and you tape on leaves."

He knew that leaves were not taped to trees. During the movie he had said, "They're not real leaves," but he repeated the movie fantasy because the idea appealed to him. It was nice to think about, and factual restrictions seemed unimportant. Since God is in charge of the way things really happen, why can't a person just think about different ideas? The child must wonder why he receives so much approval when he gives one particular answer rather than another.

At times, however, the children had no patience with magical explanations. Akemi told us she intended to plant a penny in our pot of marigolds.

Deana:	It won't work, Akemi. There's nothing in a penny.
Jill:	It can't sprout. The penny will just get hot in the sun.
Wally:	It's made of copper. It can't grow.
Ellen:	I never heard of a penny growing.
Tanya:	A penny is not a seed. Unless you put a seed *on* the penny.
Akemi:	Maybe it's a magic penny.
Everyone:	No such thing!
Wally:	She got that idea from fairy tales. Akemi, you're joking. Right?

Akemi: It really *is* magic.
(*Everyone laughs, including Akemi.*)
Wally: See? I can tell she's joking
              because she's laughing.

I thought the magic penny joke represented a significant change in the children's thinking, but I was wrong. A month later, Lisa told us she planted a penny at home and more pennies grew.

Teacher: You found more pennies in the dirt?
Akemi: Maybe the penny is magic and little
              pennies are inside and also a seed
              is inside.
Lisa: I planted three pennies and one dime.
              The next day there were eight pennies
              in the dirt.
Eddie: Maybe more pennies fell into the dirt
              before she planted and the next day
              they popped up.
Tanya: Maybe the pennies were magic and
              there were flowers and pennies inside
              the penny.
Wally: Maybe a magician dropped a penny
              into the dirt.
Eddie: Maybe God made the penny grow into
              a flower.
Teacher: Lisa, I'm wondering if someone is
              playing a joke on you. You know, like
              the joke I played with the valentine
              board?
Tanya: There's no such thing as a magic penny,
              but it *is* easy for a magician to do it.
Akemi: A magician can be outside the
              window.

Teacher:	Lisa, when you were asleep, could your brother or your parents, just for fun, have put in five more pennies?
Lisa:	No, because they were all upstairs reading and my penny was downstairs.
Deana:	Maybe someone not in the family did it. Maybe your brother's friends were flipping pennies and five of them flipped into the box and they didn't see it.
Lisa:	My brother's friends *never* play with pennies.
Warren:	It has to be a magician. Who agrees that it has to be a magician in disguise outside the window? (*Every hand goes up.*)

My valentine deception had not been entirely facetious. I wanted to know whether the children were outgrowing magical beliefs. I discovered instead that faith and principle are deliberately intertwined. Separating them would be as hard as putting the entire valentine board under Snow White.

Moving

A child's story often refocuses an event as if to view it from the outside. Characters are disguised and placed in different settings. Something that is difficult to understand in one context may seem more real in another. Whether the event is of lasting importance or merely of fleeting interest, the child seeks to dominate the experience by placing his own framework around it.

One day Wally dictated two stories: the first was prompted by his family's imminent move to a new apartment, the second by a glimpse of a water beetle in our sink.

Once upon a time a man went out to hunt and then he found a lion. He shot it for lunch and then he decided he'd make a house in the woods. So he went out to the wood stove, got some wood, got some nails, and then went back into the woods. He got all the furniture and moved it into his new house. He went to his new house to see how much room there was and then he slept in his new house. Then in the morning he shot an elephant and ate it in his new house for supper.

Once there was a little boy who lived in the forest with his mother and father and his pet water beetle. He waited in the rain for his water beetle to come inside. He said, "Come inside, water beetle!" "No, I'm supposed to like the rain. That's why they call me the water beetle."

Wally was curious about the water beetle; it may even have frightened him. But he didn't seek factual information about it. For that, he could have asked me to read the section in our big insect book about water beetles. He wanted instead a character that appeared to be a water beetle acting the familiar role of family pet.

In much the same way, Wally set his new home in the familiar forest of so many previous stories. He would not be able to control any part of his real family relocation; it would be difficult even to imagine himself and his possessions in a new place. The story, however, put him in charge of the move, right down to the nails and boards of the house. The hunter moved one day and resumed hunting elephants the next. The important things did not change.

Fred too was about to have an experience for which he had no precedent. During spring vacation he was to fly to California to visit his father and his father's new wife. He put the trip into a story that was brief and not factual.

> Once upon a time there was Snoopy and Wood-stock. They were on a trip to California. They went off the plane and went to a parade. Then they went home.

Fred knew exactly how the story was to be acted out. He directed the class to set up chairs on both sides of an aisle. He then sat in the pilot's chair, calling out information: "We're flying over Denver." "We're over China." When the plane landed, Fred passed out rhythm instruments and told everyone to parade around the room until he said, "All over. Everyone go home."

The elaborate stage directions were not unusual. Many children took their stories to be outlines; events were to *happen* rather than be read. Fred's lively scenes were a good distraction from the real purpose of his upcoming trip.

Another highly sensitive event expected during spring vacation was the arrival of the new baby at Lisa's house. Lisa had not referred to her mother's pregnancy since the day she had brought us the book about babies. However, on the last school day before vacation she dictated a story about a baby.

Once there were two dogs. They lived in a house
together. They chased a cat and ate it except the
baby pulled the dog's tail. The dog went wild. The
dog bit the baby. He ran home as fast as he could
without saying a word.

Should we assume that Lisa was expressing hostile
thoughts about her expected sibling? It would have seemed
an obvious conclusion had I not overheard Deana telling Lisa
about a frightening news broadcast. "They said on the news a
big dog bit a baby on the face. And guess what? It was the
baby's own dog!"

Lisa may have been trying to explain to herself why a dog
would bite a baby. She had a dog at home and would soon
have a baby. An adult would have said, "I wonder what the
baby did to that dog?" or "Well, you can't trust a dog." The
child acts out an explanation for a puzzling phenomenon. He
can do this in play, as he has always done, or he can use the
somewhat more formal style of the dictated story-play.

A week earlier, Lisa had invented a story to explain, it
would seem, a picture that showed a balloon coming out of a
bird's mouth. We were looking at a children's magazine in
which a robin was saying, "Here I am. And so is Spring." The
words were in a "balloon." Instead of asking why the bird
appeared to be holding a balloon, Lisa dictated this story.

The tree said, "Do you want an apple?" "Yes," said
the bird. Then the tree said, "That's enough." "But
I'm still hungry," said the bird. "Go find your own
food," said the tree. "There is a worm and there is a
balloon so what do you want to have?" So the bird
flew away without saying a word.

"Why didn't the bird answer?" I asked.

"It was a stupid question, that's why. Of course he wanted the worm. Birds don't eat balloons."

Later I explained the balloon's purpose to Lisa, but she did not make a connection to her story. Once written and acted out, a story has a life of its own. When the hunter in Wally's story built his new house in the woods, Eddie asked Wally if *he* was going to live in a forest when he moved.

"We're moving to the Kenwood Apartments," Wally answered.

"The forest is where the hunter lives."

Actors

Lisa brought pictures of her new baby sister on the first day after spring vacation. We sat on the circle, and the pictures passed from child to child.

Rose:	Does she have a name?
Lisa:	Nancy Lynn.
Wally:	Is she white?
Lisa:	I think so. I didn't see her yet. She's still in the hospital.
Deana:	She has to be white because Lisa's whole family is white. Because I was at her house. Except she has a black dog.

Wally: My whole family is black. If my
              mom has a baby it'll be a black
              baby. The only thing is we don't
              have a baby bed.
Eddie: My family is half and half. Half
              Jewish and half Christian.

Lisa studiously ignored Nancy Lynn's pictures once they
had been shown in the circle, but Deana carried them around
all day. After lunch, Deana dictated her longest story. It was
so unusual it startled the class. There was a concentrated
silence and then a sudden restlessness that was more typical
of the reaction to a new fairy tale. The photographs of Lisa's
sister had stirred up a strangely involved story in Deana's
mind and one could only guess at the symbols and clues:

Once upon a time there was a little girl. She had a
baby. Her mother said, "Take care of the baby. I'm
going to the forest to get some food." So the little
girl took care of the baby. The mother had a tiger
dress on. A hunter saw one tiger on the dress. The
hunter thought it was a live tiger. They got closer
together. The hunter shot the mother. The mother
fell down and died. Then the hunter went over to
the mother. He was just about to pick her up for
his dinner but then he saw it was the mother. So he
picked her up and gave it to the museum to show
people how she died. They wrote a story how she
died.
    The little girl said, "When is my mother going to
come back?" She went into the forest to look for
her. She followed the steps which the mother had
walked. She found a print where her mother had
been laying but she was not there. So she followed

the steps where the hunter had gone. When she got
to the museum she saw muddy steps so she followed those. Then she saw the mother dead and
she saw the story they had written. She was glad
because she had a mean mother. So she went home
and there was her father there. Her father was nice.
He gave her a piece of candy.

When I finished reading the story, everyone looked at the
class list to see which children would be first to act it out. We
kept a red thumb tack beside the last name called in the preceding story. Eddie would be the hunter. "Eddie gets all the
good parts!" Wally complained. Deana, the author, had first
choice, and no one was surprised when she decided to be the
little girl.

Almost every script turned up extra, hidden parts. In
Deana's story, besides the girl, mother, hunter, and father,
there were museum workers to make a display case for the
mother's body, and a newspaper man to print the story.

By this time the children were well practiced in improvisa-
tional skills. As in ordinary play, the actor invented appropriate lines for the part he played. Sometimes the author
wrote the dialogue, such as, "Take care of the baby. I'm
going to the forest to get some food." More often, the children spoke their own words.

Thus, when Deana's narrative read, "So the little girl took
care of the baby," Deana asked the baby, "Do you want your
bottle now?"

The narrative continued, "The mother had a tiger dress on.
A hunter saw one tiger on the dress. The hunter thought it
was a live tiger." Jill, the mother, said, "I think I'll wear my
tiger dress." A moment later Eddie said, "There is a live tiger
over there. I'll kill him for my supper."

At the beginning of the year, many children felt awkward or did not understand the idea of supplying their own dialogue. Extemporaneousness comes with practice, and three or four stories a day provide a great deal of drill. "We are like an actor's school," I told the children. "The more plays you act in, the better you'll be at figuring out something interesting for your character to say."

We had started our training with Wally's first story, which was also the first story written in the class. "The dinosaur smashed down the city and the people got mad and put him in jail."

"What did the people say when they got mad?" I asked.

"We're mad," said Eddie.

"Put him in jail," added Lisa, staying as close to the original wording as she could.

Then I read, "He promised he would be good so they let him go home and his mother was waiting."

>*Dinosaur*: I'll be good.
>*People*:   Okay. Go home.
>*Mother*:   I was waiting.

After a few weeks of cautious transposition, the children became more innovative. A story of Lisa's put across the concept of improvisation so well that from then on, most of the children needed little prompting.

>Once there was a girl who didn't like to go to her friend's house because they would always fight. And whenever they would fight, a giant would come and he likes to fight the way children do. If they fight very quiet he doesn't come. So they fought very quiet because he looked so ugly.

Lisa was the girl, Tanya was the friend, and Kenny was the giant.

Girl: I hate to go to my friend's house.
We always fight each other.
("There has to be a mother. Jill,
it's your turn next.")

Mother: You have to visit your friend. Just
don't fight. Because there might
be a giant that comes.

Girl: (Knocks on the door.) Are we going
to fight? Because if we do a giant
might come.

Friend: I know. But we always fight. So we
might as well fight. (They scream
and pretend to hit each other.)

Giant: If you fight, I'm fighting too.
(All three scream and fight.)

Girl: Okay. If you go away we won't
fight.

Friend: Fight softly so he can't hear us.
(They whisper and tiptoe as they
fight.)

Visitors were often puzzled to see dozens of stories tacked and taped all over the room, each story dated to show when it was written and acted out. The children left their stories in school if they wanted them to be acted out again. They had to wait for a day that had a light load of new stories, and the dates told us who had waited the longest.

"Do you teach reading, then?" a visitor asks. "Are these stories the method you use?"

"Not really," I respond, "although some children do learn

to read them. We think of ourselves as actors—these stories are our scripts."

Lessons

A child feels competent when he takes part in a story-play. There is just enough plot to adapt a few lines of dialogue to several fragments of action. He knows he will not be asked to do something that makes him uncomfortable. The children feel they are playing together inside a story. The author says, "Come play with me in my story," much as he would say, "Let's build a road in the block area." In both cases, the offer is taken as a compliment, a sign of friendship.

In acting out a story, the child must be more conscious of language then he is in free play. He cannot suddenly move to a parallel dialogue that has nothing to do with the plot. He can use his own words, but he must remain within the structure of the story. In addition, the stories must make sense, for they should provide directions that actors can follow. In this way a story often contributes academic lessons worthy of the best kindergarten curriculum.

In Wally's recent Snow White story, for example, the children had to solve three problems in order to act out the story: How many brothers are there? How many beds do the sisters need? How can fourteen actors (the seven boys and seven girls in the room at the time) take sixteen roles?

Here is Wally's story again.

There was a little boy with no mother and no
father. But he had seven brothers and seven sisters.
The brothers were called dwarfs. The brothers
lived in the forest and Snow White came to visit
but she didn't stay. She said, "One Snow White
mustn't live with seven brothers." So she looked
for the seven sisters. A magic bird came and took
her there. It was sixty miles away. They were glad
to see her. They ate supper and went to bed in
seven beds.

Wally:	Seven brothers . . . one, two, three, four, five, six—there's only six boys here.
Eddie:	Point to yourself.
Wally:	Oh yeah. Seven.
Teacher:	Are you a dwarf, Wally?
Wally:	No, I'm the little boy.
Eddie:	Then there's eight! Seven dwarfs and another boy.
Deana:	He could have six brothers.
Rose:	Snow White had seven dwarfs.
Wally:	Okay. I'll be a dwarf.
Teacher:	Do you need to change your story? It says, "he had seven brothers . . ."
Kenny:	Say, "He had six brothers and then he was a brother."
Wally:	No. Say, "He *was* seven brothers." (*He looks puzzled.*)
Teacher:	"*There* were seven brothers"? That means the little boy is one of the brothers.

Wally:	"There were seven brothers." Say that. Now the sisters: one, two, three, four, five, six, seven. Good. Just right. Ellen is Snow White.
Kenny:	Hey, Wally! That's just the same thing. Now there's only six sisters.
Teacher:	I could be a sister.
Wally:	Too many people aren't here.
Teacher:	What if the whole class was here and they all wanted to be in your play? Then what?
Wally:	I'd have to make it "The Twelve Dancing Princesses."
Ellen:	Where does Snow White sleep? You said seven beds. I'm eight.
Wally:	Okay. Write down: "Snow White sleeps with the oldest sister."

The difference between the above scene and "7+1=8" is the difference between intuitive learning and formal instruction. There are no numerical labels in Wally's story to interfere with spontaneous calculation; cause and effect are determined by dramatic necessity.

The mathematics was, of course, part of a larger consideration—logic. Once Wally had committed himself to "he had seven brothers and seven sisters," the words limited the action. Either the words or the action had to be changed—there could not be a contradiction between the two. Wherever Wally's words did not convey his thought, or his thoughts could not be acted out, his words had to be changed. He could not say, "He *was* seven brothers" any more than Snow White's sleeping arrangements could go unexplained.

Even so, the story-play is limited by the child's inexperience and lack of skill. To learn new words and think in more abstract ways, the children need stories written by adults. The complex plots, larger vocabularies, and wide range of characters yield an endless supply of exercises in logical thinking.

The Five Chinese Brothers by Claire Bishop, for example, appears to be overly complicated until its pattern is seen. In the story, each of five otherwise identical brothers has a unique magic quality. The first, who can swallow the sea, is wrongly accused of drowning a little boy and is condemned to have his head cut off. The second brother, who has an iron neck, changes places with the first and foils the executioner's plan. Since the second brother's head cannot be cut off, it is decided to kill him by drowning. The third brother, who can stretch his legs forever, takes his place. He, of course, cannot be drowned, so the decree is switched to death by burning. Now the fourth brother, who cannot be burned, comes forward and the death order is changed to suffocation in a vat of whipped cream. This brings on the fifth brother who can hold his breath forever. Since they cannot kill him, the people decide he must be innocent and let him go.

It was not easy for the children to remember what each brother could do or the order of their appearance, but some of them figured out that they could use either the tricks or the punishment as clues. If the first punishment is decapitation, then the second brother must be the one with the iron neck. Or if the next brother to appear is the one who cannot be burned, then the punishment for the preceding brother must be burning at the stake.

Wally realized this as he related the story. "The five Chinese brothers lived with their mother by the sea. They all had something special they could fool people with. One could swallow the sea, one had an iron neck, one had . . . I forgot what the next one could do. Wait, they threw the iron-neck brother into the sea. Oh, yeah. So that means the next one was the one who stretches down to the bottom of the sea."

There were other "lessons" in the story.

Deana:	What can the mother do? The book doesn't say what *her* magic trick is.
Kim:	Maybe she isn't magic.
Teacher:	Maybe not. But if she were, what kind of special trick could she have?
Wally:	Stretching her arms forever.
Teacher:	What could she do with that trick?
Wally:	Stretch them up to the sun.
Eddie:	No, it has to be something to trick people.
Deana:	Pretend the fifth brother was locked in a dungeon. Then she could stretch her arms and bring him out.
Wally:	Pretend they put the brother on a high mountain and he couldn't get down. *Then* she could use her trick.
Jill:	Or if he was lost in the forest.
Tanya:	No. Then she has to have magic eyes like you know in that fairy tale where the boy can see forever far away.
Andy:	Why can't *we* do the things the Chinese brothers do?
Earl:	Because we're not Chinese.
Warren:	I'm Chinese.
Andy:	It must be we're too young.
Wally:	Our neck isn't iron.

Deana: We're not in the book, that's why.
             It's a pretend story. By the way,
             where is the father?
Kenny: He's dead.

The children had other questions, for which they had
ready answers. How can you breathe if you have an iron
neck? Your breath is iron too. How can all the brothers be
magicians? Their father is a magician. What if it's all the
same brother? Then the mother would have to have more
children. Where are the sisters? They didn't like brothers
with so many tricks.

Some questions could not be answered so easily. Each time
a brother wished to return home so the next brother could
take his place, he would ask the judge, "Your honor, will you
allow me to go and bid my mother goodbye?"

"What does 'bid' mean?" I asked.

"Bite?"

"Build?"

The children began to call out words that sounded like
"bid" but made no sense in the sentence. "It means *tell* my
mother goodbye," I said, but my definition did not prevent a
further rash of incomprehensible responses as the story was
acted out.

Rose: "Do you own me to bid my mother goodbye?"

Tanya: "Can you only me to bid my mother goodbye?"

Fred: "Will you obey me to go to my mother?"

Lisa: "Can I go and obey my mother goodbye?"

Finally, Eddie said, "Your honor, can I tell my Mommy
goodbye?" and the confusion ended.

Everyone knew and used "allow," "own," "only," and
"obey"; it was "bid" that was uncertain. Once again, anticipation of the unknown confused familiar meanings.

In another story an unfamiliar word was pictured in terms so close to each child's emotional experience that a substitute word was easily found.

"What does 'people are not grateful' mean?" I asked before reading *A Crocodile's Tale*, by José Arruego.

"People are not great," Deana decided.

"Don't eat grapefruit?" asked Fred.

"No, that's not it. I'll ask again after I read the story."

The story tells of a boy who saves a crocodile's life and then finds that it is about to eat him. The boy is shocked by such ingratitude. The crocodile agrees to let him talk over the matter with a hat and a basket floating by in the river. The hat and basket each recount stories of man's ingratitude and advise the crocodile to eat the boy. The story ends when a monkey saves the boy, who shows his gratitude by providing the animal with bananas.

Teacher: After basket and hat tell the crocodile their stories—why people are not grateful—you can make up your own if you wish.

Basket: When I was new I used to carry rice for my master and fruit and then I got old so they threw me in the river. People are not nice. So go ahead and eat him, crocodile.

Hat: When I was new they used to wear me in the sun and when I got old they threw me away. So eat him up. People aren't nice.

Tanya: I'll be an old dog. When I was new they played with me. Now they don't act nice. So eat him up.

Eddie: I'm a boy. When I was a baby they
            liked me and carried me. Now I'm
            big and no one carries me. So eat
            him.

Lisa: I'm a flower. When I was new
            everyone said I was pretty and now
            I'm old so they threw me away. So
            eat him, crocodile.

Wally: Can I be someone who tells him not
            to eat him? When I was new—I'm a
            boy, too—I had to go to bed before
            "Battlestar Galactica." But now
            I'm six and my mother lets me stay
            up until eight-thirty. So sometimes
            people are nice. Don't eat him.

Deana: When I was a new puppy then they
            hugged me and when I got old they
            scolded me. People are not nice
            so you can eat him.

Kim: When I was a kitty and I cried they
            gave me milk and when I was old
            they didn't like me. Tell the
            crocodile to eat him.

Earl: When I was a baby alligator the
            people fed me but when I got old
            they pushed me in the river. People
            are bad.

Kenny: When I was new I rided my master
            around the world but when I got old he
            sended me to the horse store. So you
            can eat that boy. People aren't nice.

The children's analogies eliminated the reciprocal element
in gratitude. Except for Kenny's horse who took his master
around the world, the new characters did not perform a

service in order to receive gratitude. "People are not grateful" was taken to be "people are not nice"; grown-ups who comfort and admire babies and pets but consider five-year-olds too big to be carried are not nice. A nice parent would think his child old enough to stay up late but young enough to be carried on demand. Gratitude means responding to the child's wish.

Later Tanya said she had a story that was just like the little boy and the crocodile.

"How is it the same?" I asked.

"Because first the witches are not nice and then they are."

> Once upon a time there were three evil witches. They had a big pot full of witches' chicken soup. One heard a knock on the door. "What evil knock?" Then she went to the door and answered it. It was a little girl. The witch said, "You should get locked up in our take-time-out machine." Then the girl said, "I forgot. This is the wrong house." She tried to get out but they grabbed her. Then they had their soup. They laughed at the little girl. Then they heard another knock at the door. It was their grandmother with the witches' little boy to eat the soup. "May I have some?" asked the little girl. "Yes, you may." So the witches gave her soup and let her go free.

"Did they let her go free because she was so polite?" I asked.

"You're right. That's just the reason."

"Why is it like the little boy and the crocodile?"

"Because the witches didn't eat the little girl and the crocodile didn't eat the little boy."

Safety

The heroes of "The Tinder Box" and "The Twelve Dancing Princesses" are impulsive creatures who defy adult authority without fear of punishment. The impetuous soldier in "The Tinder Box" must have his wishes gratified immediately. Being good and bad alternately, he performs daring deeds for the witch, then chops off her head the instant she refuses to tell him why she wants the tinder box. He depletes his newly acquired wealth on candy, toys, and fine clothes and then gives away money to the poor. He orders the magic dog "with eyes as big as saucers" to capture the sleeping princess—but only for a brief glimpse and kiss before sending her back to her father.

Finally, he and the princess seize the kingdom without regret for the fallen monarchs. Unlike other fairy tales, no parental figure remains to hand over half the kingdom; the young couple gain immediate control by popular demand.

Teacher: Doesn't it seem strange that the princess is so happy to become queen? After all, the magic dogs had just killed her parents.

Lisa: She was mad at her father. He made her to live in the tower.

Teacher: He was afraid she would marry the wrong person.

Lisa: He should have just *told* her, "Don't marry any wrong soldier."

Deana: She was too lonely and sad so she didn't like her parents any more.

Wally: But she liked the soldier because

	he gave her a ride every night on the dog.
Tanya:	If they didn't punish her . . .
Rose:	Did they punish her?
Tanya:	That's how *I* get punished. I have to stay in my room.
Teacher:	What was she being punished for?
Tanya:	She was wishing to marry the soldier, that's what.
Teacher:	Did the king know she was wishing for that?
Tanya:	No, she wished it after he locked her up. See, *after* you get locked up, then you wish something bad.

"The Tinder Box" is told entirely from a young child's point of view. An older child resists some of the details enjoyed by the kindergartener. When John, Eddie's nine-year-old brother, came to class to participate in Eddie's birthday celebration, he heard me read, "What a lot of gold! He could buy . . . all the sugar pigs from the cake woman, all the tin soldiers, whips, and rocking horses in the world." John laughed and asked, "Why would a soldier spend money on *that* stuff?"

Eddie jumped to the soldier's defense. "Soldiers could like candy and toys." Then, seeing his brother's condescending smile, he added, "Or he could give it to some children."

Eddie had picked "The Tinder Box" for his birthday play and he, of course, was to be the soldier. I told John he could be in the play if he wished.

"What part could I have?" he asked.

"Be one of the dogs, John," Eddie told him. "Then you get to break everyone to pieces."

Jill, eyeing John's size, said, "Just pretend, he means."

"The Twelve Dancing Princesses" was a popular birthday choice for the girls. The beautiful sisters wear out their shoes dancing every night and refuse to tell their father, the king, where they dance. The king thinks he is punishing them by locking them in their room at night, but they have a secret passageway that takes them to an underground silver and gold forest. Twelve handsome princes row the girls across an enchanted lake to a distant palace ballroom for the nightly revel.

The story is a peer-group fantasy. The girls are sisters and the boys are brothers—all for one and one for all. No one observes the scene from the outside; each child is an insider, a full participant. This is the best of all worlds. The princesses and princes offer each other complete protection. It is impossible to punish or harm such an entourage. The only danger, jealousy, was recognized the first time we acted out the story, probably because the subject had been discussed on other occasions.

Eddie:	Sit on my rug, Deana. You can be in my boat. Okay?
Deana:	I want to be in Warren's boat.
Jill:	Warren, who do you want, me or Deana?
Teacher:	This sounds like the arguments we used to have when Deana and Jill picked certain people to act in their stories.
Deana:	Then use the list.
Teacher:	I'll make a boy's list and a girl's list and give each name a number. Then the matching

	numbers will sit together and dance together.
Lisa:	Now I don't have to worry.
Teacher:	Why were you worried?
Lisa:	Maybe I might not have a friend in the boat.

Lisa placed the princesses in several stories of her own. In one such story she included a theme from "Hansel and Gretel," but she made some significant changes:

> There were twelve dancing princesses and there was a very mean, wicked mother who said twelve is too many. So she locked her door and so they had to live in the forest. But they weren't afraid because the biggest sister said, "Don't worry. It's just pretend." Then they found a mother with twelve beds and didn't have any children. She gave them macaroni and cheese and then they watched TV.

Although "Hansel and Gretel" provided ideas for the children's story-plays, it was not a popular story. It emphasizes abandonment and fear without giving the brother and sister any protective, magical gifts. The arguments between the mother and father about the fate of the children and the punishment that follows are too real. In all of my classes, there have been children who dislike the story. This year Ellen asked me not to read it.

Ellen:	It's too scary. I don't want to hear it.
Kim:	Me too.
Wally:	It's not too scary for me. Just a little bit too bad.

Eddie:	Well, I *want* to hear it.
Teacher:	Which part is too scary? Maybe we can change the scary part.
Ellen:	Being lost and also the bad mother and father part.
Teacher:	Not the witch? Well, why don't I change the first part of the story then? There was a wicked witch who put a spell on a father and mother and made them leave Hansel and Gretel in the forest even though they didn't want to.
Ellen:	No. That's not good.
Wally:	Have them just get lost and the parents don't even know.
Deana:	They could be looking all over for them every day.
Teacher:	Once upon a time there was a poor woodcutter and his wife and they had two children named Hansel and Gretel. One day the children took the wrong path in the forest and got lost. The mother and father looked everywhere but they couldn't find them.
Lisa:	And they said, "If we find our dear children we'll never yell at them or argue or spank them ever again. We promise."
Ellen:	No. I still don't want it. Because I can remember the real words how it goes.
Eddie:	Well, I *do* want to hear it.
Tanya:	You can't, Eddie. We have a rule not to make people feel bad.

Eddie: Okay. I'll tell my mother to read
              it to me. She likes it too.

Deana's story attempted to deal with the Hansel and Gretel problem:

> There was a brother and a sister who got lost in the forest. Then they saw a box by a tree but they didn't know it was a magic box. But they picked it up anyway and carried it. The brother said, "This must be a magic box." When he said that, because that was the magic words, there came a lion. "What do you want, master?" "Take us home." So he carried them home. Then he took back the magic box in case another child got lost.

Magic that does not provide protection is unacceptable. "Hansel and Gretel" pretends to be a magical story, but it does not follow the rules. The heroes are left to their own devices, which makes them too vulnerable to offer the listener solace. The child knows there will be a happy ending because he has heard the story before, but the wait is too long without early assurances of safety. At this age, appearances matter more than facts.

Quarters

I taped the May calendar to the wall and had an instant sense of time's passage. Everything spoke to me of growth and change. Wall paintings had fewer drips, figures were in better proportion. Labels were in the children's handwriting, the letters sitting more comfortably side by side. Windowsills overflowed with bits and pieces of projects and dusty reminders of trips.

Our large bulletin board was now covered with menus, part of a complex spring project that required a high level of cooperation and coordination. The class had divided into "food committees" for the purpose of making lunch on Fridays. Each week one committee collected twenty-five cents from everyone, planned a menu, purchased food at a local grocery, and cooked and served a meal to the entire class.

With $5.75 a week to spend, the children soon figured out that meat was too costly, vegetable soup was cheaper in a mix, and chocolate cake must give way to a gelatin dessert. They also decided to grow lettuce after a member of Food Committee One pointed to a package of lettuce seeds that cost thirty-five cents. The large table, pushed over to the sunniest window, now had tiny lettuce sprouts that we would soon transplant to a corner of the fourth-grade garden.

Rose:	It doesn't look like lettuce.
Teacher:	It takes time to grow taller. By the way, it's possible the lettuce won't be ready before school is over.
Lisa:	You could bring it over to our houses.

Deana: Why can't we come here and have a party in the summer?

Eddie: When people come to this school after the summer and they'll be in first grade, then you could bring it to them.

Wally: Just give it to us in the summer if you see us.

Teacher: Would I have the lettuce with me if I happen to see you during the summer?

Wally: No. So we better all come back to school.

Tanya: We could have more school—extra school until the lettuce is ready.

Eddie: That's good.

Teacher: We can't do that. There's a summer program here, right in these class-rooms. Could we share the lettuce with the summer school children?

Deana: Give it to the fourth grade because they let us use the garden. Give them half.

Teacher: They wouldn't be here in the summer either.

Warren: Can't we take it with us?

Jill: Then you might dig up the dirt. Or dig up the seeds. You can't eat the seeds.

Warren: Just leave it here until it grows. Give it to the summer school kindergarten. I mean, some of it.

Eddie: Give them *all* of it. Let's just *buy* lettuce. It's not too much expensive. Anyway, how do we know it's really lettuce?

Teacher:	The label says "Bibb Lettuce."
Eddie:	What if it's really tomatoes?
Teacher:	Oh. Are you wondering about the picture of tomatoes with the lettuce on the packet? It's just an idea for a salad, after the lettuce comes up.
Warren:	They might think they're lettuce seeds and they might not know.
Earl:	Maybe the seeds look the same as something else.
Teacher:	Do you think they could make such a mistake?
Lisa:	Just bring it back to the store if it's wrong.
Deana:	The store people didn't even make it.
Eddie:	You have to take it back to the gardener.
Deana:	Maybe they printed a word they wanted to spell the wrong way. Maybe they mixed it up.
Eddie:	They could have meant to put different seeds in there and then they turned around and went to the wrong table.
Wally:	The wrong part of the garden. The tomato part.
Warren:	So in case it's not lettuce it could be tomatoes.

There was no suggestion of robbers or magicians; human error was the only factor considered. The ideas for distributing the lettuce crop were equally practical. Certainly there was no reason to believe that the school year could *not* be extended to accommodate the growing season, nor were the children being unrealistic in assuming, in this age of freezers, that we could save the lettuce until first grade.

In contrast they were stymied by the problem of giving Akemi change for a dollar. We had fifteen quarters taped on our name chart when Akemi brought a dollar.

Akemi: My mother says bring her the change of the dollar.
Warren: Ask your daddy for a quarter.
Teacher: We have all these quarters here. We can give Akemi change. How many quarters did we say equal one dollar?
Everyone: Four.
Lisa: She can go to the bank.
Rose: Her mother has to go. Not children.
Eddie: I'll ask my dad. He's got a box of quarters for the parking meter.
Teacher: But look at all these quarters. (*Silence*) Look. Here are four in a row. Earl, Kim, Lisa, Mickey. If you four make change for Akemi, we'll just pin the dollar across all your names instead of your quarters. Then how many quarters will we give back to Akemi?
Eddie: Four.
Teacher: Okay. Akemi, here are four quarters. You can tape one up by your name and bring three home to your mother.
Kim: Do I have to bring another quarter?
Teacher: No. The dollar includes your quarter.
Mickey: Do I have to bring a quarter?
Wally: We can all give them quarters.

> *Teacher*:   The dollar is the same as their four
> quarters. Just pretend Earl, Kim,
> Mickey, and Lisa still have their
> quarters up there.

My explanation was not convincing. Everyone had memorized the equation: four quarters equal one dollar. However, these particular quarters belonged to four distinct children. I said the quarters had turned into a dollar, but the children involved felt a sense of loss. On Thursday when Kim's committee untaped the quarters and unpinned the dollar in order to go shopping, Kim examined the dollar and said, "Where's my . . .?" She left the sentence unfinished.

The following week I provided a jar for the quarters and asked the children to list their names separately. Later I showed them a dollar.

"I had no quarter at home. What should I do?"

"Put in your dollar and take out four quarters," Eddie told me, "and then put in a quarter."

"Do you all agree that it's fair?" I asked.

Everyone nodded.

"Kim, does it matter which quarter I take?"

"It doesn't matter," Kim answered. "They're all the same quarters."

Two weeks later the children decided they preferred the quarters taped next to their names. "You can remember better if you brought your quarter," someone said. This time Eddie needed change for a dollar, and the confusion was repeated.

> *Jill*:   I don't want my quarter to be change.
> *Teacher*:   Didn't we decide that all the quarters
> are the same?

Jill:	I like to look at my quarter. Can't Eddie's mother go to the bank tomorrow?
Teacher:	No, but Eddie can go to the office for change, if he wants to.
Eddie:	Yeah. I want my own change.

Ladder

The children still leaped to unrealistic conclusions when items suddenly appeared or disappeared, and often they accepted changes without seeking any explanation. Therefore, when an eight-foot horizontal climbing ladder was delivered to our room one day in May, I did not call the custodians or rearrange the furniture or print a list of safety rules. I waited for the children—not for reasons of democratic procedure but rather to strengthen shaky connections and to infuse a sense of purposefulness into the physical environment.

Teacher:	I expected this ladder to be delivered last September, when you first came to school.
Wally:	Why do you need it? The one outside looks just like the pictures on the box.

Teacher:	Sometimes it's too cold to use that one. Remember all the times we couldn't go out?
Rose:	And when it rains.
Teacher:	Right. Also we'll get more exercise if we have a ladder in the room. Shall we try to put it together?

(*I open the carton and remove pipes of various sizes, wooden poles, and packages of bolts and screws.*)

Eddie:	I can do it easy!
Deana:	Don't let him! Then it'll fall down. Ask Mr. Prentice.
Wally:	Leave it alone, Eddie. This is for a workman to do.
Eddie:	I might be a workman when I grow up.
Teacher:	I'll send Mr. Prentice a message. Meanwhile let's decide where to put the ladder.
Warren:	In the blocks.
Andy:	No! Then how can we build if people are swinging?
Wally:	Hey! Guess what? That's a great beanstalk for Jack. Put the ladder in the circle.
Rose:	Even for the three billy goats it's a bridge.
Akemi:	The soldier can climb down to get the tinder box. Also the funny little woman.
Teacher:	I never thought of that. I only thought about exercise.

Wally: We can do exercise too. Hey, I'm
going to do a story with the ladder.
After Mr. Prentice comes, I mean.

Mr. Prentice assembled the ladder the next day, while we
sat on the circle and watched every step. I read the directions
aloud, and he let the children hold parts and bring him tools.

Wally's vision of the ladder as an extension of our stage did
not surprise me; the children often saw possibilities that I
missed. Our perspectives were necessarily different—my
thoughts were on safety, while Wally imagined a magic
beanstalk in the air.

The general approach to putting up the ladder was another
sign of progress. Eddie's automatic "I can do it easy!" was not
copied. Nor did anyone suggest climbing into a crane sus-
pended from the ceiling. This job required precise adult
skills. Eddie quickly withdrew his offer and substituted a
future goal: "I might be a workman when I grow up."

The children now had a more realistic view of what they
were capable of doing. In the fall they would ask for help in a
simple task but insist that they could fix a broken table. Now
they were more likely to plan something they could complete
themselves, rather than begin work on a hopelessly difficult
task, such as Eddie's plan in October to build a closet for his
father's birthday.

Eddie had collected wood for a week, storing it in his
cubby. "First I'll make the door," he told everyone. On
Friday he came to me and insisted I help him. "I can't do it by
myself. It's too hard!" There were tears in his eyes and blame
in his voice.

"Choose a present you can make yourself, Eddie."

"That's no fair! You *have* to help me." Now he was really crying.

"I can't," I said. "I don't know how to make a door, Eddie."

Wally came over. "Why is Eddie crying?"

"He's angry because I won't help him make a closet door for his father."

"Why won't you?"

"Even if I knew how, his father would know Eddie didn't make it."

Wally considered this for a moment. "Can't you do a smaller present, Eddie?"

"Like what?"

"A boat."

"That's not a good present."

Deana, coloring nearby, overheard the conversation. "Make him a tiny table like the kind I made for my teddy bear."

"Okay," said Eddie, still scowling as he went to the woodworking bench. By the time he had sawed four sticks and glued them to the corners of a four inch-square of wood, he was in a better mood. "Anyway," he concluded, "if I had more better pieces of wood I could make a door easy."

In May, Eddie was no longer building closet doors. Since midyear most of his hammering and sawing had involved computerized weapons and exotic communications devices for his superheroes. In my search for signs of change, I had to be careful of superheroes. With his newspaper cape and mask, Eddie appeared much as he had in September, and a teacher might overlook the considerable evidence of growth.

Magical thinking is not all of one piece; it increases in some areas and decreases in others. A comparison of two discussions, eight months apart, revealed strong evidence of growth in realistic thinking. Both conversations were about Leo Lionni's *In the Rabbitgarden*, a story that makes subtle fun of superstitious thinking. The story tells of two bunnies who are warned by an old rabbit that if they eat from a certain apple tree a fox will get them. When the bunnies run out of carrots, they are given apples from the forbidden tree by a friendly serpent who then saves them from the fox.

In October I had asked Eddie and Wally if eating the apples brought on the fox.

Teacher: Why did the old rabbit think the fox would get the bunnies if they ate an apple?

Wally: He owned the apples.

Eddie: The fox liked apples and he thought they would steal them.

Teacher: What if there were no apple tree? Would he still try to eat the bunnies?

Wally: It wouldn't make any sense to say it if the apple tree wasn't there.

Eddie: He didn't want to share the apples.

Wally: If they ate it and the fox saw it, he could get them. Here's a good trick. The fox invited them for dinner and if they ate one apple he could eat them up.

Teacher: Would the fox eat the bunnies *because* they were eating his apples?

Wally: It must be. If it isn't that, what else could it be?

Wally and Eddie were unable to imagine any connection between the fox and the bunnies besides the words of the warning. The fox will eat the bunnies only if they eat the apples. To support this notion, the boys decide that the fox owns the tree, though the book gives no information about the fox.

When I reread the story in May, ownership of the tree was still a factor, but the children were able to see beyond the tree to consider the natural inclination of foxes.

> *Teacher*: Why did the old rabbit think the fox would get the bunnies if they ate the apples?
>
> *Lisa*: It's the fox's apple tree and he doesn't want anyone to touch it.
>
> *Teacher*: How do you know it's the fox's apple tree?
>
> *Lisa*: The fox growed the tree when he moved there. It takes a long time for apples to grow so he didn't want anyone to touch his tree.
>
> *Wally*: Foxes like to eat bunnies and also it took a long time to grow the tree.
>
> *Teacher*: Would the fox get the bunnies because they were eating the apples?
>
> *Wally*: He might still try to keep all the apples to himself.
>
> *Teacher*: What if the bunnies hadn't eaten the apples?
>
> *Earl*: Maybe they couldn't reach them.
>
> *Wally*: Well, he still might have tried to eat them because foxes in the forest, if there's any rabbits around, they *do* eat them.
>
> *Deana*: Foxes like to eat rabbits best of all.

Fred: If the bunnies can't reach the apples
           then what if the fox doesn't get them?
Deana: He doesn't want the apples. He wants
           the bunnies.
Wally: He'll just keep chasing the rabbits
           until one day he gets them.
Kim: If it's winter and the apples are gone
           he'll be hungry so then he'll keep
           chasing them even more.
Wally: Here would be a good trick! The fox
           takes out all the carrots so they
           can't eat carrots. Then the bunnies
           have to come to his apple tree where
           he's hiding. Then he can jump on
           them. It's like a trap.

Between October and May the apples on the tree had lost some of their power; foxes eat rabbits with or without apples. Instead of a reason to eat the bunnies, the apples are a lure to capture them. This was the same realism that doubted Eddie's ability to put together the new climbing ladder. The children had a better perspective on both Eddie and the apples.

Carrots

Another pair of discussions resulted from a story written by
Wally to celebrate the climbing ladder.

> A little boy planted a carrot seed but he didn't
> know it was magic. So the next day there was a
> huge carrot growing up to the sky. And it had little
> bumpity places so you could climb up. Then he
> saw a giant. But the giant didn't see him. When the
> giant fell asleep he stoled a magic tinder box that
> gave you food if you were hungry. Which was a
> very good thing because his family was poor and
> didn't have any food. When he climbed down they
> had a party because it was also his birthday but he
> didn't know it.

"Wally, is that the same little boy from the carrot seed
story?" Rose asked.

"No, it's a different boy."

"Remember everyone kept telling the other little boy it
wouldn't come up? They shouldn't do that. They have to say
it will come up or it's not polite. And remember the giant
carrot?"

Rose ran over to the bookcase and found *The Carrot Seed*.
She held up the book. "Now we can have a discussion."

The book by Ruth Krauss had been read on the first day of
school. It is the briefest of stories, about a little boy who
plants a carrot seed. Everyone tells him it won't come up, but
the boy waters it and pulls the weeds daily until one day a
giant carrot comes up.

Our discussion in September had dealt with the points

Rose referred to in May: the response of the family and the size of the carrot.

Teacher:	Why do you think the family tells the boy it won't come up?
Eddie:	Because he plants it in the sand.
Wally:	He can't wait so long. He waited too long. So it *would* come up.
Earl:	Because if they were saying it so long he'll keep pulling up the weeds.
Warren:	They didn't have to tell him because I knew it would come up.
Jill:	He planted it in dried-out dirt.
Rose:	Boys don't even come there.
Wally:	She means to plant things there.
Jill:	If he keeps watering, it will come up.
Warren:	If they keep *telling* him, it will come up.
Deana:	Why is the carrot bigger than the boy?
Eddie:	Because they weren't looking.
Wally:	He watered it too much. He didn't know how.
Jill:	Some carrots grow this big.
Teacher:	Bigger than a boy?
Eddie:	He planted too many seeds.
Wally:	Or he watered it too much. *And* he put in too much seeds and they got stuck together. Or maybe it's a giant's carrot.
Lisa:	An underground giant.
Wally:	Giants are in the sky. Only they grow their carrots in the ground.

By the spring I had forgotten how much younger the children had sounded in September. In May they seemed more mature in every way, as the Friday lunch project showed. Yet in literary matters, magic still prevailed.

Teacher:	Why is the carrot so big when it comes up?
Warren:	It was in the ground too long.
Rose:	What if the seed was too big?
Eddie:	Like if it had some small pieces of plant food in it.
Wally:	They put many seeds together to make the carrot bigger.
Fred:	Maybe he had a lot of carrot seeds and he wanted a big carrot.
Wally:	It could be a magic carrot.
Eddie:	A plastic carrot.
Teacher:	How could a plastic carrot have gotten into the ground?
Deana:	He just dug it in and it grew because it was magic. Maybe someone stoled the small carrot and put a big one in instead.
Teacher:	Who?
Rose:	When he was sleeping.
Kim:	How could the robber find a big carrot if they grew a small one?
Eddie:	Maybe someone put a plastic carrot in the ground for the one that was stolen.
Deana:	How did they find the place where the little carrot was so they could dig it up?
Eddie:	The robber found the sign with the

carrot on it and he had his flashlight and he dug around.

Fred: How could he see? He can't hold
the flashlight while he's digging.

Eddie: He puts it down while he digs. Then
he puts a big carrot in and takes out
the small one. Then he puts the sign
back.

Deana: And he smooths down the ground.

Wally: Wait. Here's a good thing. The robber
could go underground himself in the
hole and then he could feel the roots
and pull them out. See, he digs a
tunnel from his house to the carrot
and pushes the carrot over. He takes
the real carrot and puts in a plastic
one.

Tanya: The boy will know it's plastic.

Wally: Not if it's a magic seed. As soon as
the boy picks it up, it turns into a
real carrot.

Rose: Why is the giant carrot red?

Teacher: Oh. I can tell you that. You see,
the book only uses three colors—
brown, tan, and red. So they make
the carrot red. The more colors you
use when you print a book the more
it costs.

Eddie: If it's a magic seed, then it *would*
be a red carrot. Red is a magic
color.

Lisa: Unless it's food coloring.

Magical solutions were still acceptable; the children were
more inventive and carried ideas further, but the direction

was unchanged. My brief allusion to the economics of printing was washed away by the image of red as a magic color. I had never heard that red was a magic color—perhaps no one else had either—but Eddie's statement was accepted as a fact.

Earl's second-grade brother Harry visited us just after the *Carrot Seed* discussion, and Earl told him about the magic seed and the clever substitution of carrots by a robber. Harry said, "That's really weird. Boy, Earl, you're really weird."

After Harry left, I said, "Earl, your brother doesn't agree with you about the giant carrot."

"That's because he doesn't like carrots," Earl explained.

I was not surprised by Harry's disdain for magic seeds and robbers who steal carrots. I would not have expected a second-grader to think along those lines. Yet I wondered whether other kinds of magical thinking persisted in the second grade. Harry seemed so grown-up when he visited us—until he began to play. Then he entered the world of Star Wars and Superman as if he had never left kindergarten. Similarly, Lisa's sister, also a second-grader, could barely wait to get into our doll corner before saying, "I'll be the mother."

Suddenly I had a great urge to ask Harry's class about mother lions and magical powers. I talked it over with Harry's teacher, who offered to read to my class while I taped a discussion with hers.

> *Teacher*: A kindergarten boy once told the class he intended to become a mother lion when he grew up. He said he would do this by practicing magic.

Thalia:	Magic doesn't make things that people want to be.
Teacher:	Is there any use for magic at all?
Thalia:	There are magic tricks. You can learn tricks.
Harry:	Well, he could put on a disguise and then there could be a tape recorder beside him of a lion and people would think that's a real lion.
Thalia:	But that would still be a trick.
Stuart:	Like the magic set my sister gave me. The balls don't really disappear. They're in the cups all the time.
Harry:	The only kind of magic there really is is superhuman strength. Now *that* really is true.
Allan:	If you know how to do a magician's things, you do have to keep practicing until you know how to do it real good.
Thalia:	But it's still just tricks, Allan.
Allan:	Everything isn't tricks, Thalia.
Teacher:	Even if you practiced for years, could you learn to become an animal?
Allan:	No. But maybe something else.
Stuart:	My friend does this—it's not magic but it's like magic. Like once he believed so hard his father would give him something and when that day came his father really gave him what he believed.
Teacher:	Is that like wishing?
Stuart:	No. He was just believing in his mind that his father would give him something.

John:	That boy in your class. It was just something he really wanted it to happen but it couldn't happen. It was a fantasy.
Harry:	Scientists could work hard and make up a formula to make someone into a lion.
Thalia:	The only kind of magic I've heard of are miracles.
Teacher:	Is that something like Stuart's friend believing in something real hard?
Thalia:	A little different. Like you're wishing something will happen but you know it won't and all of a sudden it happens.
Sally:	I think there might be a potion some day. I don't think it could happen, I mean a potion to make someone a lion. But it might happen.
Harry:	They might be able to not make him into a lion but make him look like a lion with all the doctors working hard to do it.
Sally:	You mean to look like a lion but not talking like a lion. Not roaring or anything. But it wouldn't be magic. It'd be something to do with science.

These doctors and scientists sounded a bit like the kindergarten magician who stands outside windows changing ordinary pennies into magic ones. Harry and his friends spoke of fantasies, miracles, and potions, keeping a safe analytical distance. But between the lines there was the possibility that changed appearances constituted some kind of reality, that wishing might still guarantee an outcome, and perhaps above all, that superhuman power was attainable.

One day while trying to move the piano, I was reminded of another illusion of superior power.

"I can't seem to move it," I complained. Wally, Earl, and Deana began to push with me, but the wheels refused to turn. We called Jill to join us, and this time the piano inched away from the wall.

"This is like *The Tale of the Turnip*," I said. "Do you remember?"

Everyone remembered the story of the grandfather, grandmother, grandchild and black cat who cannot pull up an enormous turnip until a little brown mouse comes to help. I wondered if the children still credited the mouse as the chief agent of the move.

Teacher:	Why did the turnip come up?
Tanya:	The mouse is so strong.
Deana:	All those people were there. So the brown mouse came and there were more people.
Jill:	There were more people so it was too hard to keep it in.
Earl:	I think they're all pretty strong so if they all pull it out it'll come out fast.
Rose:	The mouse was holding on to it. He was holding the roots.
Wally:	He must of seen the roots underground and he climbed up to see what it was so he tried to push it out because he's stronger.
Kim:	The mouse's place was under the

	turnip. So first he pushed it up. Then he crawled around and pulled the cat's tail.
Tanya:	Children aren't so strong as parents, and old people aren't strong because they're too old. The cat wasn't that strong but the mouse was stronger than the cat.
Eddie:	But there were too many people pulling it so when the mouse came it might have just slipped out.
Warren:	The mouse and cat are stronger because they're younger.
Wally:	He could of been right under the turnip in a secret place and then he could of chewed it and pushed it a little and also when the people kept pulling and pulling it got looser and looser.

Wally teetered between the practical reality of people pulling together and the vision of a powerful mouse. Later I asked, "Remember before, when we tried to push the piano and it wouldn't budge? Then Jill came to help us and it moved. Is she stronger?"

"We only just needed a little extra help," Wally answered.

"Everyone helped the same," Jill said modestly. They knew it took our combined efforts to move the piano, but they were not quite sure about the turnip and the mouse.

"Did everyone help the same in pulling up the turnip?" I asked.

"Yes," said Fred. "But not if the mouse has superpower."

"Does he?"

"Maybe he does." Fred tried to read my face. "Maybe not the one in the book. Maybe a different one."

Jill came to his assistance. "He means like if there was a real giant turnip and a real supermouse—not in a book."

They were telling me that they knew the author did not intend the mouse to be a supermouse, but that such a phenomenon could exist. An idea could be examined on two levels: the obvious fact seen by the adult and the possibilities seen by the child.

Girls and Boys

Besides elevating children's moods and expectations, the superhero theme declares their differences as boys and girls. Nowhere is this separation of interests more clearly maintained than in their stories. Many family and magical themes are used by both girls and boys, but the most obvious differences lie in the boys' overt use of physical force, contrasted with the girls' emphasis on family serenity. Boys exult in superhuman strength, girls seek gentle relationships. Boys talk of blood and mayhem, girls avoid the subject; a character in a girl's story simply dies, no details given. Boys fly, leap, crash, and dive. Girls have picnics and brush their teeth; the meanest, ugliest character in a girl's story goes on picnics and keeps his teeth clean.

Boys narrate superhero adventures filled with dangerous

monsters, while girls place sisters and brothers, mothers and
fathers in relatively safe roles. If lost, they are quickly found,
if harmed they are healed or replaced. Boys tell of animals
who kill or are killed; girls seldom involve animals in
violence. A bear or lion encountered in the forest is likely to
lead a girl home and will not be shot and eaten for supper.

The plot of a girl's story often revolves around the friendship of two little girls who play and sleep together; I find no
examples of little boys who are friends and do nothing but
play. A friend is a superfriend, and the proper activity for
superfriends is making trouble for bad guys. The most ordinary little boy kills lions and does not visit the playground.
Certainly he will have nothing to do with the queens and
princesses who inhabit the girl's forest.

Girls tell of beauty, love, and marriage, as in the fairy
tales. Boys enjoy the same fairy tales but will not include
such material in their stories. Phrases such as "fell in love" or
"got married" embarrass them. They are more comfortable
with "put him in jail" and "broke through the bars."

I had continual opportunities to observe these characteris-
tics, for story-telling became the central activity of each day,
taking up so much of my time—as well as the time of student
teachers, aides, and visitors—that I tried to call a temporary
halt.

"I have an idea and I think it's a good one," I told the
children one day in early spring. "There are a number of
games you would all enjoy, but I haven't had time to show
them to you because of the stories. So, starting with next
activity period, let's stop the stories for about a week. Okay?"

There was a general nodding of heads while the children
looked at each other. Then suddenly there was a stampede to
the story table—crayons, paper, and pencils flying.

"I was first!"

"I got here before you."

"That's my seat."

"You didn't take a number."

"Because your hand was on it!"

"Hold it!" I shouted. "I changed my mind. I didn't realize so many of you were about to do a story. Let's just keep going the way we were." In a day or two we were back to the normal rate of four to six stories a day. I did not again suggest a hiatus. It was as if I had said, "Tomorrow I'm closing the block and doll corners. Finish up all your play now."

During the last week of school, there was a flurry of superhero stories. Even Wally, who seldom mixed superhero play with story writing, dictated a series of Spiderman adventures, all variations of his first.

> Captain America and Spiderman were in jail. Captain America broke the bars. Then Spiderman and Captain America got out. Then the other superheroes came. Then there was a boat. All the superheroes got on. Then a wave came with a shark. Then the shark tried to bite Captain America but it missed. Then the shark tried to bite Superman. Then Captain America beat up the shark. He said, "Watch out. Stay back." Then there was a sign in the water: "Don't pass." They passed to see what it was. A water devil was in it. All the other superheroes wanted to go home because they were scared but not Captain America and Spiderman.

For Eddie the theme remained constant.

> There was once some superheroes. And there was Spiderman and Batman. All the other superheroes

were dead. Spiderman and Batman got on their motorcycles. And Spiderman saw them dead on the ground. He got them all alive. Then he said, "All superheroes go away except Batman and me will stay here." The lions came to bite them. Spiderman and Batman beat them up. Then they went home. They slept until next morning. Next morning there was no trouble.

Earl introduced a new character into our cast of monsters.

The Creature of the Black Magoo

Once upon a time there was a ship. It was night time. Everybody was sleeping inside the ship. There was a princess there. Then two ugly hands came on the boat. It was the Creature of the Black Magoo. He took the princess underwater into a cave. Then it was morning. Then the people in the ship woke up. They saw the princess was all gone. A man on the ship got in a diver's suit to go find the princess. He went underwater in a cave where the princess was. While he was looking around, the Creature of the Black Magoo grabbed his neck and choked him. He died. Then the Creature of the Black Magoo broke the ship all up. He ate up the princess. A policeman shot him but it didn't hurt him. A policeman came and took him to jail. Then he broke out of jail. He bit the policeman and he died.

"Why do only boys do superhero stories?" I asked.
"I'm going to do a superhero story," said Jill.
"Me, too," Lisa added.
"Girls don't," Wally told them.

"Girls can if they want," asserted Lisa.

Lisa and Wally were both right. Girls can but they don't. They watched the same programs as the boys and seldom refused a part in the boy's stories, but they did not initiate superhero play or stories. Nor did they behave in these stories as the boys did. An all-boy cast choreographed a ballet in continuous motion. The presence of girls slowed down the physical activity and decreased the sound effects, for the girls used none of the code words or ritualized movements.

Jill and Lisa, determined to tell superhero stories, gave us two doll-corner stories in disguise.

> Once upon a time Princess Leia, Stormtrooper, Darth Vader, R2-D2, Obi-wan Kenobi, C-3PO went for a picnic. They went back home. Then they went out for lunch. They ate supper, went to sleep, got up, brushed their teeth, and went for another picnic.

> Once upon a time there lived a rocket ship on space. All the little kids used to have fun on the rocket ship. There were Martians there who were bad and the little children rescued them and put them in jail. Then they had more fun on the rocket ship.

"There are so many superhero stories lately," I said during lunch.

Deana knew why. "They just love them to pieces. The boys want to think about them all the time. They don't ever want to be daddies."

"It's better than daddies," said Eddie. "You can think

you're a real superhero. Then you can be strong. Daddies can't be so strong."

"Don't girls want to be strong?" I asked.

"Girls want to be mothers and sisters," said Fred. "They do house stories."

Deana objected. "Mine are palace stories. Not house stories. Princesses and queens live in magic palaces."

"Are superheroes magical?" I asked.

"Some know magic and some don't," Wally said. "Joker does and Spiderman does."

"All the ones that fly do," Eddie decided. "Other people can't fly except in a plane."

"They can break through walls," Warren reminded him. "That's magic too."

"My dad says those walls are cardboard," said Eddie.

"I know," Warren agreed. "I'm talking about when it's real walls."

Deana was firm. "They're not magic because they're not real. They're on television."

"We're talking about real superheroes," argued Eddie. "With superhuman strength."

As if to prove that she did not tell house stories, Deana dictated a story with themes from at least six different fairy tales.

> Once upon a time there lived a princess with her mother and father. They lived in the forest. Then one day the mother said, "Go into the forest." And so she went into the forest. She picked some strawberries and blueberries until she came to a little house. She knocked on the door. Nobody answered. So she opened the door. She was so tired that she lay down on one of the beds and fell asleep.

When the old lady come home and saw the pretty girl fast asleep she decided to take her for a walk. So when she woke up they went for a walk. When they came home the old lady was jealous because she thought the princess was much prettier than her. So she said, "Go out in the forest and get me some shiny red apples." So she went into the forest and she looked but she couldn't find any shiny red apples. She was lost.

Then she saw a hollow tree. She went into it. She was so tired she went to sleep. When she woke she fixed up the house and when it was all finished she got a basket and went out looking for something to eat. Then on the way she met a prince. They decided to get married. And they did. And they went to the king's palace and lived happily ever after.

Then the queen had a baby. The baby was a girl and that was the princess's sister. Then the mother needed a babysitter. The babysitter was jealous because the princess was prettier so she put the princess to do all the work. Then when the mother caught the princess doing all the work she said, "You'd better not make her do all the work." But the babysitter did not listen. One day when the princess was sleeping she woke her up to do the work. The princess ran away to a new palace and became the queen and married another prince.

I had a few questions for Deana:
"What happened to her mother?"
"She died."
"What happened to the first prince?"
"He died."

"And the sister?"

"She died—also the babysitter."

"Why does everyone die?"

"It's a magical story. They don't have to stay dead. Except bad people have to. Everything with a princess and queen is magical."

"Boys feel that way about superheroes," I said.

"No. Superheroes are pretend—not magic. They're just saying that. Magic is really alive. I mean it's invisible. Super-heroes are like putting on a costume and thinking you're one."

I asked Wally if he agreed with Deana.

"She's right," he conceded. "Only God decides about magic. Superheroes don't have to do with God. Unless he wants it."

Even without their names at the top, I would have known that all the stories told on the last day were by girls. Ellen's could never have been dictated by a boy.

> Once upon a time there was a beautiful fairy. Her name was Jennifer. She had a father and it was a king. They loved each other very much. Then the fairy made her father the king into a beautiful prince. The prince and the fairy loved each other too. They decided to have a celebration and they got married.

Nor could Fred's story, a week earlier, have been a girl's.

> Speed Racer crashed into the wall but he still keeps going. Then he explodes Racer X and he catches Racer X on fire and he explodes Fire Fox and he wins the race.

Tanya and Jill dictated our final stories. In each one a parent is in need and a child goes out into the world to bring back a treasure. Having made the brother her hero, Tanya decided to take that part instead of the customary sister's role. Even in this respect girls were different. On occasion a girl would give herself a boy's part, but boys avoided female roles in their own or anyone else's story.

> Once upon a time there was a little girl. She lived with her mother and brother and they had no money so the mother said to the little boy, "Go out and find some money." He went. Then he said goodbye to the little girl and his mother. He found some money in a wallet in the woods. He ran home. He told his mother, "I found some money in the woods." They were all glad. The sister danced around for joy.

Jill listened carefully to Tanya's story and decided to give the little girl a stronger role.

> Once upon a time there was a little girl. She lived in a cottage with her daddy. Her daddy said one day to go out and find some fruit and bring it home and we would be able to eat. And so the little girl did it. When she came home she brought a whole basket of fruit. And he loved her best of all because she brought him a whole basket of fruit and never asked for any money.

"Can I do a story?" Wally asked.

"I'm sorry, Wally. There's no time left." I pointed to the clock.

"I'll do it tomorrow."

"This is the last day, Wally."

It was suddenly very quiet around the circle.

"You'll start writing your own stories in first grade, you know," I said.

The children looked surprised and then pleased. But I felt lonely.

Appendix

Each year I come closer to understanding how logical thinking and precise speech can be taught in the classroom. These skills are, I believe, the important precursors to formal schooling and the main business of the kindergarten teacher. The book describes my search for the child's point of view with which I can help him take a step further. In this appendix I upstage the child and talk about the teacher.

The skills involved in rational discourse require much practice. The teacher, therefore, must use material that children want to discuss and dramatize. Fortunately, such topics are easy to come by, for anything that affects the child's status in the classroom, with particular emphasis on friendship and fantasy, will receive his attention. But that attention can be fleeting, appearance and form changing with the twirl of a Superman cape. The teacher must help the child see how one thing he knows relates to other things he knows.

In the following discussion the children are willing to concentrate on a problem because they want to affect its outcome. My task is to keep the inquiry open long enough for the consequences of their ideas to become apparent to them.

Teacher: Yesterday I asked Warren and Earl to share a cubby so we could get rid of the old section of cubbies. You know Earl is the only one still using it, and we need

the space to store our wood supply.
But then Eddie and Wally said *they*
wanted to share a cubby. And Deanna
got upset because she asked Lisa but
Lisa had already asked Jill. It's becoming a big problem.

Eddie: I think we should do it because last
night I couldn't sleep. Just because it's
not fair about Warren and Earl.

Lisa: It is a little bit fair because we need
more room.

Deana: What if *I* can't sleep?

Lisa: Why doesn't everyone share?

Mickey: I don't want to. It's too crowded.

The cubbies will certainly be too crowded, but that is of
little importance to most of the children—or to me. I would
not have created such a problem, but it is real and it touches
on many deep concerns: friendship, security, fairness. In the
discussion I act as the ancient Greek chorus, seeking connections and keeping track of events, but the decisions must
come from the children. This is not to be merely an academic
exercise.

Teacher: We have at least three problems here.
First, should I have asked Warren and
Earl to share a cubby just because we
need more space? Second, can others
decide to share even if it hurts someone's feelings? Third, what if some
people don't want to share at all?

Eddie: If a person says to share my cubby
and if the other one doesn't want to,

	he doesn't have to. Or if the first one doesn't want to.
Tanya:	Maybe you can't find someone to share.
Lisa:	I would be a good sport and share with you.
Jill:	That's not a good sport. You said I'm your partner.
Wally:	It *is* fair because you just say she promised you first.
Rose:	No one promised me.
Teacher:	Mickey doesn't want to share and Rose thinks she won't have a partner. How can we tell if she'll be left out?
Eddie:	Let everyone sit by the one they want.
Teacher:	Okay. We'll see if anyone is left out. (*There is a noisy scramble but soon everyone is seated.*) I count four groups of three, four groups of two, and Kim and Mickey are alone. So that's three, six, nine, twelve who don't agree on partners.
Warren:	The extras can go with the extras.
Deana:	Jill can go with Tanya.
Jill:	I'm not extra. You're extra.
Teacher:	How do we know who is extra in a group of three?
Tanya:	It could be who is the shortest one.
Jill:	No! That hasn't got to do with cubbies! "Shortest" is when someone has to crawl through the window to get the key.
Teacher:	What *does* have to do with cubbies?
Lisa:	Whoever asks first.
Fred:	Best friends.

> *Deana:*   But how about if three people are best
>   friends? That reminds me. Why can't
>   we pick our own actors to be in our
>   own stories?

Any sudden switch in topics is a challenge for the teacher,
who must try to find a common element between the new
idea and the ongoing discussion. This is done not to soften
the children's non sequiturs but to demonstrate logical connections. In Deana's case the connection is fairly obvious,
but even when the teacher's reasoning is incorrect, the children witness the process by which such inferences are made.
To dismiss a statement as being "off the subject" forfeits a
valuable teaching moment.

> *Teacher:*   I think I know what reminded you of
>   that, Deana. Choosing your own ac-
>   tors *is* a bit like picking a cubby part-
>   ner. Let's talk about that after lunch.
>   Right now we must decide about the
>   cubbies. How about the children who
>   will be disappointed? How many
>   people can we allow to be sad before
>   we say it's no fair?
> *Deana:*   One person.
> *Jill:*   No. That's not enough. Because you
>   could only just be in a bad mood from
>   something else.
> *Deana:*   All right. Half the class.
> *Teacher:*   How many is that?
> *Wally:*   When *you* say, "Half the class goes
>   to music," is that the same as half
>   the class?

Teacher: Yes.
Wally: Then that's eleven because Red group
           has eleven.

This is a good place to mention the tape recorder. I missed the implications of Wally's "Is that the same as half the class?" until I transcribed his comment from the tape later in the day. Then I was reminded of Lisa's, "Are you really Mrs. Paley?" Is "half the class" an arbitrary label, Wally wondered, or is it the same "half" he already knows? The class was divided into two groups, Red and Blue, because only half of the children could attend music at one time. My occasional references to "half the class" came across to Wally as code for "group." He knew that each group had eleven members and was called "half the class"; I had been satisfied with this reasoning until I heard the tape. His asking if "half the class" meant *half* the class showed that he did not visualize a numerical meaning for half of twenty-two children. He could break a cookie in half, draw a line through a circle, and divide six blocks at a glance, but he could not *see* half of a large number.

Subsequent activities revealed that others were also uncertain about this concept. Lisa, for example, told us that if you don't know a group of people you could ask them their names and divide them into half and put half on each half of the circle and then count up to eleven and that would be "half the class."

Lisa's complicated statement tells something about what she knows and doesn't know. However, before I can weigh this information, four hands are waving, Tanya is fussing with Rose, and Earl's brother comes in with a message from their mother. Luckily the tape recorder preserves everything.

It has become for me an essential tool for capturing the

sudden insight, the misunderstood concept, the puzzling jux-
taposition of words and ideas. I began to tape several years
ago in an effort to determine why some discussions zoomed
ahead in an easy flow of ideas and others plodded to a halt,
and I was continually surprised by what I was missing in all
discussions.

I now maintain a running dialogue with each tape as I
transcribe its contents into a series of dated notebooks. The
margins fill with unasked questions. "Does Lisa mean that
half of any class is automatically eleven, or does 'count up to
eleven' describe the *process* by which a group is divided
equally?" reads one marginal note. Another states, "Her 'ask
them their names' refers to my question: how can you tell
what *half* is if you don't know the class or how many children it has?"

The tape recorder trains the teacher, not the child, who
never listens to the tapes and who is curious about the
machine only the first time. The teacher learns to watch for
inexactness in her questions, to repeat a child's inaudible
comments, to ask for clarifications and additions. The initial
incentive for these changes in style may be her desire for a
more useful tape, but she soon realizes that whatever
produces a better tape also achieves a more articulate discussion.

"Mickey, when you say 'Put a block in the middle and then
you'll know which is half,' what do you mean 'in the
middle'?"

"Like ten over here and ten over there and then a block in
the middle."

The continuity a teacher looks for in her curriculum can
often be found on the tape. For this reason I own only one
cassette, which forces me to transcribe material the same day

it is produced. Many a new discussion begins with a statement like this:

> Teacher: I was thinking about what Tanya said yesterday: "You put one on one side and say 'one.' Then one on the other side and say 'two.' Then one on the other side and say 'three.' " Tanya, could you show me how that's done?

Step by step, the children and I can follow a train of thought, giving those who need more time the opportunity to reflect. And the teacher is there to make connections.

> Teacher: So, if eleven children are disappointed, we forget about sharing cubbies. Okay. I'll sit way over here. When I call you, come and whisper the name of the partner you want. Don't tell anyone else the name and I won't either, so no one is hurt.

Concentration is intense. The discussion is now thirty minutes old, but there is no sign of restlessness, although a few children have gone over to take something out of or put something into their cubbies, as if to reassure themselves that nothing has changed.

The children are silent as I tally the results of the whispered choices. I put X's on the board under two labels—a smiling face and a sad face. There are twelve in the sad column. I cannot assume, however, that everyone understands the meaning of the two groups of X's. The sudden appearance of an abstract symbol can be a distraction.

Teacher:	Why am I using X's instead of your names?
Rose:	X's and O's.
Teacher:	The X *is* like the one in the game. There it tells which box you picked. What does this X tell?
Kim:	Who you picked for a partner.
Teacher:	It tells something about who you picked.
Jill:	If you picked someone and she picked you then your face is happy. But it has to be a secret.
Teacher:	Right. So we use X's instead of names. Are there too many sad faces? (*Everyone agrees.*) Then we all keep our own cubbies.
Rose:	Even Earl?
Teacher:	Are they sharing because they're friends?
Lisa:	They *have* to share. That's not for being friends. That's for doing a favor to the workbench.

During the activity period that follows, Deana is the first to dictate a story, one whose origin is clearly the cubby incident. My role as scribe is never passive; wherever possible, I enlarge the scope of the story, looking for points that need clarification and asking questions that might lead to new twists in the plot. My goal, however, is as much to give children practice in exposition as to improve their stories.

Once there was three children. They were princesses and one of them was a queen.

"You said 'three children.' Was the queen a child?"
Deana looks surprised. "No. I mean the children are acting

out a story. Me and Lisa and Jill. Jill is the queen and she sleeps alone. Me and Lisa are the sisters and we sleep in the same bed."

"That sounds like sharing the same cubby."

"It is. No one else can ever come in our bed because we're the only two sisters."

"All right. So there are two princesses and a queen."

And then the first princess met a prince who was magical. He turned into a funny dragon because he wanted to get married to a princess. She said, "No." She went back to Strawberry Hill where she lived. The end.

"Did she know the dragon was a prince?"

"Of course."

"Why did he change himself into a funny dragon?"

"Because he wanted to make her laugh. But she wasn't marrying someone just because he made her laugh."

"That would be good in the story."

"Okay."

So when she went back to Strawberry Hill her sister asked her if she met someone in the forest and she said she met a dragon that was really a magic prince and he wanted to marry her but she told him, "No." So she said, "What else can you be?" And he said, "A handsome prince." So he did.

"Wasn't he already a prince?"

"Oh, yeah. I forgot."

Now the sister was happy because before the magic prince was so ugly. That was why he changed to a

funny dragon. So then she said, "Can you become
two handsome princes?" So he did and the two
princesses got married and went to get a bridal
shower.

"What's a bridal shower?"
"I don't remember."
"It's a party for someone who's getting married. Everyone
gives her presents."

Then the magic prince gave them a baby called
Princess Small One and they didn't have to make a
wish and wait for the baby because it was a
present.

When Deana is finished, I ask, "Shall we do the story after
the discussion?"
"Yes. Because then I can pick Lisa to be my sister."
In the afternoon we take up Deana's objection.

Teacher:	Deana wants story writers to choose their own actors. Who remembers why we started using the class list to give our parts?
Earl:	Some people didn't get a turn too much.
Tanya:	Then everyone is in a big fuss and they'll always be saying I didn't get picked neither and then it'll never stop and nobody'll ever get picked the whole time they're in school.
Teacher:	Tanya thinks people will be jealous and keep arguing. That's why we began using the lists.

Deana: Let people always pick different
              people. Not the teacher. A child has
              to do it.
Eddie: Or if you don't get picked write your
              own story.
Warren: But if people aren't fair let everyone
              tell them to be more fair. Tell them
              who didn't get picked yet and they
              have to pick that one.

As the discussion continues, more children go over to Deana's side, which is seen as the one opposite to the teacher's position. The vote is unanimous in favor of the rights of authors. I am not surprised. The morning's decision left a number of children feeling dissatisfied and, as Deana knew, there *is* a connection between sharing a cubby and sharing a story-play.

The hours of this day were tied together by a continuity of mutual purposes that transcended play, but wandered not far from it. For play is the natural response of children, with its own logic and consequences, and deals often with the same problems of possessiveness the class struggled with today.

I do not ask the children to stop thinking about play. Our contract reads more like this: if you will keep trying to explain yourselves I will keep showing you how to think about the problems you need to solve.